# Marriages

## of

# Destiny

# Kathy Laity

## (with Philip Laity)

published by

**PrintWorks**

published by PrintWorks©

First published in Great Britain in 2012

© Philip and Kathy Laity 2012

# DEDICATION

I dedicate this book to my parents, Bill and Eileen Ruddock, who celebrated over 40 years of marriage and to my step-dad Eddie Salloway, who came into my life after my father died and married my mother when she was 70; adding great happiness to her latter years and a further 10 years of marriage, as well as being truly a second 'Dad' to me .

Thank you all for modelling to me marriages which worked, even through the tough times and led me to believe in the lasting, life-long commitment of one of God's greatest gifts to all people everywhere.

Thank you,
your daughter,
Kathy


I dedicate this book to my parents David and Eileen Laity, who have been married over 60 years and have supported and loved me throughout my life. Thank you particularly to Mother for her example of faith and prayerfulness, through the ups and downs of life. Thank you to both of you, for your many acts of kindness and generosity to me over the years and now to Kathy too. It's a joy to see you both enjoying the autumn years of your marriage, in contentment and companionship.

Thank you,
your loving son
Philip

See! The winter is past:

The rains are over and gone.

Flowers appear on the earth;

The season of singing has come,

The cooing of doves

Is heard in our land.

The fig tree forms its early fruit;

The blossoming vines spread their fragrance.

Arise, come, my darling;

My beautiful one, come with me.

**Song of Songs 2 v 11-13**

# CONTENTS

# PART ONE

Above all else, guard your heart, for it is the wellspring of life.
Prov 4 v 23

Seek the Lord while He may be found; call on Him while He is
near....for My thoughts are not your thoughts, neither are your
ways My way, declares the Lord. As the heavens are higher than
the earth, so are My ways higher than your ways and My thoughts
than your thoughts. As the rain and the snow come down from
Heaven, and do not return to it without watering the earth and
making it bud and flourish, so that it yields seed for the sower and
bread for the eater, so is My word which goes out from My
mouth: it will not return to Me empty but will accomplish what
I desire and achieve the purpose for which I sent it.
Isaiah 55 v 6 - 11

If the Lord delights in a man's way, He makes his steps firm;
though he stumble he will not fall, for the Lord upholds him
with His hand.
Psalm 37 v 23-24

# Life Before There Was An 'Us'.

## *Kathy*

One night, I had a dream which changed my life. I watched my 'ex fiance' (the man I loved) marrying someone else. I was crouching at the back of the church sobbing, my heart broken. On waking, I felt the Lord whisper 'If you don't let him go, this will be you'. Now, I recognised the Lord's voice, even though I knew the girl in question was engaged to someone else. What could I do? I let him go and began grieving for what would never be. I was in my early twenties and already beginning to feel the first bump along the road, in the journey to marriage.

It's through these bumps that I learned something of God's heart for the marriages of His loved ones. In this book, Philip and I have openly shared our courtship, which started with a 52 year old bachelor and a 44 year old widow, so that we can now pass on to you some of the lessons we have learned.

The book is written to openly reveal God's dealings in our lives and we believe our story may provide keys enabling you to move forward into marriage. It is written for those who are waiting, maybe disappointed along the way, needing fresh insight or renewed courage.

Before we really get going, let's pray together.

*Father, we come to You on behalf of our readers who are desiring marriage. We come boldly knowing You love marriage and You take great pleasure in bringing people together. We pray for those who are hurting, that Your Holy Spirit would heal the pain and enable faith to rise once more. Lord, in the waiting period, we pray that You would draw near and reveal the greatness of Your love for them individually. Please use this book to unlock the destinies of many people and enable them to move forward into marriage. Expose the enemy's interference in their lives when he seeks to thwart Your plans. We ask it humbly in Jesus' name. Amen.*

Throughout the book we highlight lessons we have learnt along the way. What lesson did I learn from this dream?

**Lesson Learned**

**When God spoke, I had a choice. Either I could believe Him at His word and obey, even though it wasn't what I wanted and was painful, or I could disobey but face greater pain down the road. I had freewill to choose. God wasn't going to make the decision for me.**

Over the following weeks, I relinquished that relationship, realising this was the end and that even friendship was impossible. Naturally, I was sad, confused and emotionally raw.

Then God caught me by surprise because the last thing I was looking for was another relationship. At the time, I was working in a Christian outreach centre and one evening I was paired with a young man, Geoff, to do street evangelism. However, it was a Monday, pouring with rain and there wasn't a single person out and about. We ended up spending the whole evening sheltering in the doorway of Marks and Spencer, talking….and talking…..and by the end of the evening we were firm friends.

We both felt the connection; the ease with which we talked surprised us. Over the next few months we 'bumped' into each other all over the city, unexpectedly. If I tried to be somewhere I thought he'd be, he wouldn't be there but if I let go, then I'd meet him. I had no control over the meetings, nor did he. It was as if God was supernaturally arranging when and where we met.

I was desperate not to make the same mistakes I'd made previously. I couldn't face that kind of hurt again and my heart was quite vulnerable. I'm sure many of you understand what that's like. So I was prayerful about this relationship, asking for God's guidance at every step, not just imploring Him for my will to be done. I wanted His will!

One evening we were at a missions meeting where an evangelist was speaking. I wasn't particularly interested in being a missionary, as I loved my church and the city I was living in, expecting to stay there for the rest of my life. However, that night, God spoke loud and clear to me, through a vision and into my heart that He was calling me to be willing to 'go' into all the world and preach the gospel. I was sitting next to

Geoff when God said, 'And I want you to let go of him'.

I was devastated. I ran out of the meeting crying. What could God be asking of me? Didn't He know I'd already had a broken heart and I hadn't looked for this relationship and now He was asking me to give it up? Was I confused! Emotionally I felt my world had been turned upside down and fears of every nature started shouting loudly. For a while, I listened to them but once my emotions calmed down, I prayerfully came before God and rather reluctantly applied for missions training. But I was perplexed, especially over the guidance I thought I'd received. I let Geoff go, explaining what I believed God was saying to me, even though by then my heart was his and I was again in love. He also agreed to let me go, recognising God was at work in my life.

It was six months before my training started yet our paths continued to cross. We would still end up meeting 'by chance' despite our efforts to avoid each other.

This situation was putting considerable strain on us and we needed God's help, so we decided to fast, to seek Him for clarification. At the end of this time, we both sensed He was giving us back to each other. Jeremiah 29 about God's good plans, marrying and settling down, kept coming to my attention. This didn't mean all was straightforward. I then went away for my missionary training and a time of separation, which lasted 8 months, with very intermittent contact.

This particular mission didn't permit relationships during training and you needed permission when on staff to date someone. So, every obstacle imaginable was in our way. Months went by and I was posted to Denmark, then New York. We met briefly for one weekend after about 6 months apart but there was nothing but barriers in the way and I can remember him saying 'I feel about this relationship like a soggy hamburger thrust in my face', hardly encouraging! We both very nearly walked away at that point, yet I knew God had spoken. Finally, when Geoff was taking me to the bus station at the end of the weekend, for me to go on and fly out to New York, he suddenly said 'I think we should make a go of this relationship'. Not brilliant timing. We would again be apart with no means of contact. This was in the days before mobile phones and emails!

But God intervened! After months of being in different parts of the world, we finally met up, realising we still had feelings for each other. Prayerfully, we agreed to begin to rebuild our friendship even though I was in London and he was in Sussex. We managed to meet up weekly on a Friday evening, walking the streets of central London, exploring the sites, sipping cups of tea and enjoying each other's company. It was a fun if somewhat unusual courtship.

For over 16 months it had been a 'push me-pull me' situation with us never knowing when or how we could see each other. Thankfully, with the help of a senior leader's wife who recognised that the mission organisation was keeping apart two people that God was bringing together, we found ourselves living on the same base. Bless her. She saved us! Within 8 months we were married.

However, during that time I was talking with one of the older married women in the mission and pondering why Geoff and I were the only couple, who had made it through to marriage. There had been several other couples engaged but who broke up. She was the first person to enlighten me that there is a battle over Christian marriage. She shared how she was praying regularly for the assignment to be broken over our mission, so that people would meet and marry. (After all we were mainly young people from all over the world in our twenties, wanting to marry). I noticed that once Geoff and I were married, a door seemed to open and many others followed. It's as if something shifted in the heavenly realm and a trail had been blazed for that season, which allowed others to follow through in our wake. We weren't special, we just persevered, believing God had spoken and I know prayer was going up on our behalf.

### Lesson Learned
**God led me to lay down any right I felt to marriage. It was like Abraham being willing to sacrifice Isaac. He didn't know that Isaac would be returned to him and was willing for him to die, even though God had promised many descendants. Laying down a right is the same. We have to be willing for God to take it totally, as a sacrifice. I had no idea God would lead me back to Geoff. When I gave up the relationship, as far as I was concerned I walked away and would never see him again. It feels really tough at the time but**

we do it, just like Abraham did, trusting in the wonderful nature of our God – who is loving and kind above everything and who has our interests very much at heart.

Also, during the time when I was tied up with my missions training, we could have looked logically at the circumstances or even our feelings and decided the relationship was going nowhere. We could easily have ended it but had we done that, we would have stepped out of God's best will for us. The bottom line was, He had already spoken that He was bringing us together and He'd confirmed it. Whose voice would we listen to: His voice or our own? Thankfully, and I'm sure with His help, we hung on in there and followed His leading. Looking back, I'm quite amazed it didn't fizzle out, especially as both of us had other people who were keen to be closer to us – a further temptation!

Just on that note. I do think that had we not followed through on the relationship, God would still have redeemed our situations. If you are reading this and think, oh no, I've blown it with someone. Take heart. God is able to work out a different plan and work with every mistake we've ever made. He can still lead you to someone and them to you. It doesn't mean you've only had one opportunity and that's it!

I believe prayer and contending for our marriage, declaring and believing what God had already said, played a big part in us eventually marrying.

So, the convoluting ways of how I met and married Geoff were very much led step by step by God. I learned to follow the Lord's leading and I'm so glad I did. I've also learnt that the enemy is very active in stopping the people of God coming together. If I'd paid any attention to his various blockades (emotionally, mentally and physically) and not listened to God's voice, I doubt we'd have married.

By the way, my ex fiancé did marry the home-group leaders' daughter, 4 months after Geoff and I were married, (just as I'd seen in my dream - see page 8) so if I hadn't listened to God, I would have been standing at the back of the church broken-hearted. Instead, I was happily married and the news barely registered except to rejoice for them.

So, Geoff and I married and we were together for nearly 14 years, through great times and some really tough times. Our marriage ended suddenly, in the blink of the eye, when he was killed outright in a road traffic accident and my life went into freefall, with only the everlasting arms of the Lord underneath me. (You can read about this in my book 'Inside Grief' written for those walking through bereavement).

My automatic reaction when Geoff was killed was to run to the Lord (not away from Him). I knew that I wouldn't get through unless He helped me.

I remember vividly how He kept prompting me to read the Book of Ruth during the time between the road accident and the funeral. Normally I'd have turned to Psalms for comfort but it was as though God was saying, 'stay in Ruth, I'm speaking to you'. And Ruth is all about a widow marrying an older protector provider, Boaz, after a terrible time of suffering. I began to recognise that God was already speaking to me about remarrying. I was fairly incensed. The husband, best friend, lover that I adored wasn't even buried and here was God speaking about remarriage. How insensitive! Yet..... I knew His prompting, gentle, insistent and clear.

I didn't want to remarry, certainly not initially, in those early ragged months of grief stricken pain but I was young, still in my thirties and gradually as the months moved into years, I realised that I did want companionship again and I really missed being a wife. Geoff and I had discussed remarriage if either of us died. We had freely given our permission to each other, to do so. This meant I didn't have the feelings some widowed people have of betrayal or guilt at moving on.

However, the months after Geoff's death were harrowing. I was torn apart emotionally and physically as my body bore the brunt of the shock and trauma of his death. I was laid very low with physical ailments which led me to lose my job. Life was bleak. I was living alone, ill, very lonely and with no work. But above all, I missed Geoff with every fibre of my being. He'd been my soulmate, my best friend, my prayer partner, my strength, my companion, the one I ran to at the end of the day to be hugged, the one who gave me confidence. I loved him, deeply. Loneliness enveloped me and looking back I realise I gave in to self pity too. I wasn't sure I was ever going to emerge from this dark tunnel. God was close, yes but there were days when the pain was so intense I would collapse on the floor, hugging my knees and just rocking. It was grim.

Why include this? I wanted to show that I too have hit rock bottom and provide hope. If God can bring me through something as dark as this, He can bring you through your season of trial and struggle. But also, I want you to know I understand the pain of the heart and that the words I write I want to be from compassion and not in any way condescension. There are some very bleak seasons which some of us have to walk through, hand in hand with God. I encourage you to keep talking to Him. He always responded to my absolute honesty. He could take my anger, my accusations, my pain, my angst and then He'd come and wrap His love around my heart and bring comfort.

Now there were several things which happened in my years of widowhood which I found interesting but puzzling. When married, Geoff and I had been in church leadership positions, accepted in our church circle and part of what was going on. Immediately I was widowed, it seemed to change. Somehow others were awkward around me. I realise now that most people don't know how to deal with tragedy and therefore tend to avoid you, rather than asking how they can help. But from my end, it felt like married people in particular, found me invisible. Life became very lonely, except for my wonderful single friends.

During our marriage, Geoff and I had always had many unmarried friends as part of our little extended family and so when I was widowed, this seemed perfectly natural to continue. It just shocked me that not many married people included single people in their social circles. It was quite revealing for me. It contributes greatly to a loneliness in our church families, which grieves me. If you find yourself one of those feeling on the outside, I just want to say I'm sorry, on behalf of married people, for not noticing and not including you in the very centre of church life. Thankfully, there are many churches where this isn't the case but where it is, it needs to be acknowledged and the hurt faced up to. Also, if any of you are or have been on the receiving end of this behaviour, I would urge you not to hold grudges and to resist falling into self pity. We have to be pro-active and change where we can but accept that people fall short and need our forgiveness. Bitterness is very unattractive, so please, don't let it get a hold and if its tentacles are already gripping you, repent and let God take it and pour in His healing.

Anyway, after a year or so, with no man on the scene and living in a very rural place, I found myself wondering what I could do to meet single Christian men. I'd already been corresponding on the internet with a widower who I'd emailed when I learnt about the death of his wife in a car crash. He was with a missionary organisation and in the US, so I was awake and contactable when his world was asleep. Knowing the insomnia of grief I'd 'be there' for him in his darkest hours and we built a lovely friendship. God led him miraculously to remarry swiftly but it left a hole of male friendship in my life and that's when I thought about trying out the internet Christian dating sites.

This was an illuminating experience, in many ways positive and in others a bit disconcerting.

I certainly believe that God does bring people together through these sites and am not of the opinion that you must sit back and wait for God to do all the work but I say that on the proviso that *prayer* and *guidance submitted to wise counsel*, is the foundation of all action. Whatever route God takes people on to meet, this must be the prerequisite, before emotions, feelings, and mutual attraction take over. Once these are awakened, it's really very hard to hear what God is saying and be objective about the situation.

So, I started corresponding with several people, initially only in the USA. I think I was placing a barrier deliberately, to keep people at arm's length. Then I met up with one or two people in the UK. It was clear though from their reactions that a 40 something lady, who was short and cuddly was not what most were looking for. Be encouraged ladies, God led me to someone who was not influenced by this.

So, the dates were somewhat varied but not totally enjoyable and I often emerged with a very battered sense of self worth. I'm being honest here. At times it was excruciating going through this process and I respect the courage of anyone who goes down this route. It's not easy. I think your own confidence and knowledge of how loved you are by Jesus and others, eases the process, but any insecurities will inevitably surface.

I also joined The Network, which is a social Christian organisation

*Don't get sidelined by circumstantial evidence*

where you meet other singles but on excursions or special interest days and I went to their New Year 3 day party. It was great. It catered for extroverts and introverts, with a whole variety of activities and I met some really great Christians, both men and women. It was far less intense than meeting one on one and allowed for more natural interaction and friendships to emerge.

At this point, I'm going to add in a bit of a side story because it was a whole episode where circumstantial evidence might have again led me down a wrong path.

I'd been corresponding on a Christian website site with a number of men in the USA. I had a work related conference coming up in the States and imagine my reaction when one of the men started asking where the conference would be held. It turned out it would be a couple of hundred yards from the university, where he was working! Could he meet me and show me around? The odds of this happening were immeasurable and now I was in a spin! Was God up to something?

How 'coincidental' this was and you've guessed it, I started running ahead in my mind. We'd certainly got on well by email and had some overlap in both our professional and personal lives. It seemed logical to meet up. I was sensible and did this in a public place in our hotel before agreeing to spend the day with him. It went really well, though I didn't particularly find as much common ground as I'd expected – but I was definitely trying hard to find it!

The conference was soon over and I headed to the airport but my plane was delayed 24 hours. I had the option of staying where I was or having 24 hours alone at Newark airport, which I really didn't want. I was alone and knew just this one person – so I rang him. He arranged accommodation for me, and transport to and from the airport. And still I was thinking God was up to something. As it turned out He was! He was ensuring that His daughter was safe and cared for in a foreign land, full stop.

But I pushed it, thinking there must be more because of all the circumstantial evidence. I invited him to visit the UK and it looked hopeful but then the delays started. The emails dropped away and six months later I received an unexpected announcement of his marriage.

**Lesson Learned**

**I learnt so much from this. If he'd encouraged me by coming to the UK, I'd have jumped, so eager was I to remarry. Also, I would have read God's hand into the circumstantial guidance. There had been no other confirmation, not least from scripture. Above all, I believe because of a prayerful heart, God actually prevented the relationship from progressing because we weren't right for each other, however much I was trying to convince myself. What a comfort, that God overruled here. As I trusted Him, He prevented me from making a wrong decision.**

Part of me had expected to remarry swiftly, because God had spoken so soon after Geoff's death. In reality, it was several years before anything happened. I was not enjoying the website experiences so gradually it let it fizzle out. If I did remarry, it would have to be to someone as committed to Jesus as I am and their walk with God was more important to them, than I would be. Those were my criteria really. I was willing to relocate, even around the world and I didn't have my checklist at the ready – I know it works for some, but my reasoning was that God knows me better than I know myself. He knows the type of husband I need, as well as want. He also knows the man for whom I would be a blessing and gift. I'd let Him do the choosing.

## *Philip*

As you will have already realised, my journey towards marriage was very different from Kathy's but no less God directed. Whereas she wanted to be married and prayed along those lines, it was as far from my thoughts as could possibly be imagined. I was now into my 50s and believed I would remain single. In fact, for various reasons, I felt certain I was called to be single.

In my teens and twenties I had courted several girls. I tended to be attracted to slim blondes with long hair; but although I was fond of them, I never fell in love and felt no real emotional attachment. However, I was also confused. I'd been sent to a mixed boarding school when I was 10 and because I was very slim and lanky (my language would be skinny and bony) I was teased about my body. I was useless at most sports which unfortunately for me, was a major focus of the school. As a result of teasing, I began to reject my body and became jealous of muscular well built men, almost idolising their physique. I wanted to be like them and this opened the way for me to become very confused about my sexuality. Also, I felt inferior to my father who was more solidly built and excelled at several sports.

Whilst growing up on a busy farm, much of the time my father was out on the land working very hard. This meant most of my upbringing prior to boarding school was left to my mother. The result was a very strong bond with her and a much weaker connection with my father. I received little physical contact or affirmation from him which left a deficit of male nurture in my childhood. This in turn led to a weakened sense of my own masculinity. However, I did have a grandfather living with us, with whom I had a close bond and this brought in some balance.

So, I grew up trying to 'fit in' on the girl scene but also feeling an occasional stirring towards men and gradually I began to believe the lie that I was not to be married but remain single and celibate. This view was reinforced by wrongly believing that the following scripture applied to me; 'For some are eunuchs because they were born that way; others were made that way by men; and others have renounced marriage because of the kingdom of heaven. The one who can accept this should accept it', Matthew's Gospel chapter 19 v12. I'd never fallen in love, didn't feel I needed this in my life and was happy being independent. I didn't even know I was lonely, I was so unaware of my emotions and shut down. However, I didn't always appear this way to others.

During my adult years, despite my own thoughts, there were several women who wanted to marry me and some even approached me with proposals. Rather than reject them outright, I would take them out to test the relationship and also seek God for His leading. I realise, since being married to Kathy and having my emotions reawakened, that I hurt some of these women very deeply through my brokenness and caused pain for which I'm really sorry. However, at the time, I was acting out of my rationale and logic. Sometimes I wouldn't even know

Peace

Turmoil – Is it God's guide or our weakness?

the women were interested in me, or that inadvertently I appeared to be encouraging them. I was very naïve about the ways of women and how they interpret a man's attention. I'm much wiser now. So when a relationship caused me to be uncomfortable or created inner turmoil, I would back out and feel justified in doing so. I literally was unable to understand that I was causing deep pain.

Having said this, I did know that a good way of knowing God's guidance is the measure of peace experienced inside. So it wasn't just my own inexperience with women, or wounds which caused me to back away, but the divine hand of God. It's as if the closer I would get to someone, the more inner turmoil would surface, to the point I would be very near an emotional breakdown and traumatised. Part of this was caused by inner wounds in my soul which needed healing and also the surfacing of issues around fear of intimacy. I needed to distinguish between whether I was losing God's peace, or if there was an area that required healing. They were two separate issues.

Hence there was a real battle going on in my life over marriage. I was fairly naïve in my communication and I would love to bring some of the wisdom I have learnt to other men here. Women believe what you say. If you are talking about marriage, they will assume you are talking about them and not generally. They then often run ahead in their minds and see themselves married to you and setting up home.

The inner peace or turmoil was a major indicator for me of God's leading and so when on a number of occasions Christians would approach me and say they really weren't comfortable that a certain relationship was of God, I valued their counsel and it would usually confirm the inner turmoil I was feeling. I don't want to dishonour any of these Godly ladies, so will leave it at that.

So here I was, in my early 50s, not having been in a relationship for many years and with very troubled memories of the last experience, which was deeply traumatic, leaving me reluctant to even contemplate a further relationship. I had firmly shut the door on marriage and barred it with bolts. It was then that God decided to intervene and my world went into a whirlwind of change.

# The Point of Meeting

**Trust in the Lord with all your heart and lean not on your own understanding; in all your ways acknowledge him and he will make your paths straight.**
**Prov 3 v 5,6**

## *Kathy*

So, this is where I found myself 4 years after Geoff's death, pretty much resigned to being single and though I knew I'd heard God about remarriage, not at all in faith that it would happen. I had begun to look more at my circumstances and let them dictate what I thought, than hang on to the things God had been speaking to me for those years. I won't pretend I wasn't lonely, I was. I won't pretend that I was living a fulfilled single life, I wasn't. I was miserable, even though I had great friends. I had loved being married and I missed it. I can remember a prayer time though where I seemed to come to the end of myself and my efforts. I laid the whole marriage thing down, placing it firmly back into God's hands to resurrect if He wanted to. I decided to trust Him and let it go.

I tried to immerse myself in my work, church and friends. I was part of a fellowship setting up 'Healing Rooms' and was due to go through the training. (If you want to know more about Healing Rooms, please see the resources appendix). Healing Rooms are where people can come off the street for prayer for healing. It operates pretty much like a doctor's surgery but without the appointments. I was very excited about this venture, firmly believing that God is in the business of healing today and longing to reach out to people through this avenue.

Ironically though I was ill, the week of my training and stuck in bed. I'd decided not to go when I heard a clear whisper 'Get up. Go to the hairdresser. *He* will be there'. I just knew, with that inner knowing, that God was referring to my husband being present at the Healing Rooms training.

I was a little startled and not totally believing I'll admit but I was obedient. I went to the hairdresser and I went to the training, walking in on the first meeting, to be greeted by rows of grey heads. I chuckled with the Lord 'Well, I know you said he'd be a Boaz but really!' Remember, I was still only early 40s and not ready for a husband years older than me! I sat down on a pew in the middle on the right side. Half way through the first session, a man sitting near the front turned around and smiled directly at me. It was a wondrous smile, a smile that connected, that seemed full of joy and light. I felt a faint stir inside 'that's him.'

'Well, who's him?' I wondered waiting to see what God would unfold and if I truly had heard Him.

I didn't get to meet the 'man with the smile' that day. The next day our training continued. We were going to apply the training we'd learnt in practical sessions and this required us being in groups of four. I was attending with two dear friends, who sat down on a row next to 'the man with the smile'. When we split into groups of 4, they invited him to join us. I was a bit startled! They knew nothing of what was unfolding. In our practical, one person was prayed for, another led the prayers and the final two prayed silently. I ended up being prayed for by 'the man with the smile'! I could feel his hands on mine and remember them feeling just like Jesus. I felt safe and this was amazing because God was dealing with some deep grief issues that day.

I looked a mess, crying and feeling wretched as God dealt with my pain but it didn't affect the outcome at all. God started what He wanted to do. By now you'll have guessed that yes, this was Philip. I swiftly realised that here was a man of enthusiasm which I found greatly attractive and a passion for Jesus which was compelling. He'll be telling his part of this story but will add that my friend Cynthia, who was part of the little group and knew I wanted to remarry, came up to me afterwards saying 'I've a feeling about you and this Philip. Do you want me to do a bit of detective work and find out if he's single?'

Philip, at this point, was totally oblivious to the fact that God was setting him up.

**Lesson Learned**
**God orchestrated our first meeting at His appointed time. There**

was a set time because we've since learnt that we were present at the same events, the same conferences, had friends who we both knew, yet we'd never met. We'd been skirting around each other for over 10 years!

I went home full of joy, wondering what would happen next and knowing that I should do absolutely nothing. I didn't know anything about Philip except he lived in Cornwall and was running a Christian centre at the time. I lived in Devon. At least we were in neighbouring counties. We didn't talk privately, didn't even connect other than during the prayer time and over lunch.

So, I waited and wondered.

**Lesson Learned**
**It's important not to chase or manipulate situations but to have faith and trust in God to work things out. We listen for the quiet prompt of the Holy Spirit's nudge. When we get involved doing it our way, it gets messy and someone usually gets hurt.**

## Philip

I went to the training for 'Healing Rooms' because I was fascinated by the concept and already involved in a healing ministry. On the second day of the training, we split into groups for practical work. I was with Kathy and her two friends, as she's explained. Whilst ministering to her, I saw an inner picture. I'm not naturally prophetic so only receive them occasionally. I shared the picture with her - it was of a very large, very beautiful bouquet of wedding flowers, in whites and creams and totally gorgeous. I thought it was a beautiful encouragement from the Lord, saying that she was His bride and how much he loved her. I didn't see the significance of the picture for some months. Kathy however, because the Lord had already told her about our relationship, realised immediately that it was a confirmation but very wisely didn't say anything to anyone but let God do His work.

When I met her again a couple of weeks later at another training event, we went for a walk at lunchtime for some air. I am much taller than her, 6'1" to her 5'2" and I walked in the gutter and she on the pavement, so we could look more directly at one another. This fact showed in a funny sort of way, that I wanted to engage with her. I admit I felt an attraction then, and enjoyed her company and vivaciousness but nothing more. I certainly wasn't admitting anything else to myself.

**Lesson Learned**
**Listen for the quiet prompting of the Holy Spirit and don't let your mind argue you out of what you've heard Him say.**

## Kathy

After this second meeting, I left with nothing to go on, except the still small voice of the Lord. I had to wait, to pray and above all trust God and not try to manipulate or drive anything forward. If God was bringing us together, He would have to do it.

So, imagine my surprise when just six weeks after first meeting Philip my home-group decides to go away on retreat to his Christian centre in Cornwall. I'd caught in my heart the vision which Philip had shared about a healing centre, where God's glory was present and people came to be healed and helped. So I was really excited about going. And what a weekend we had! It was a time of immense joy and celebration for our little group. From time to time I'd see Philip around and would be so aware of him, it was like charged electricity!

**Lesson Learned**
**God doesn't need my help, He's well able to ensure things move along.**

On the Sunday at Philip's church, I can remember vividly, worshipping and feeling some kind of spirit connection with him. It seemed as if our spirits were one. It was so strong and felt so right. That afternoon we ended up going on a long walk along the Cornish cliffs together. The sun was shining, the sea at its bluest and it was the most magical walk. We laughed, shared, talked easily and I thoroughly enjoyed his company. Fish and chips in Fowey ended the day, with a jackdaw hopping along the sea wall, periodically pinching our chips – possibly the first 'sign' we had from God. You see, every date, every walk, every time from then on that we were together, there was a 'sign' in the natural realm, usually birds (because I love wildlife) or rainbows. I remember the little jackdaw, so does Philip. He made us laugh at his audacity.

Our friendship had begun and I hadn't had to do a thing, except be obedient and wait. It's hard to explain but I felt already that I belonged with this special man, who I was made to complete, to love and minister to for the rest of our lives. It was that clear I wrote this in my journal – yet we hardly knew each other in real terms. I think I'd just recognised him for who we were meant to be to each other in God's plans.

On leaving Cornwall, I still didn't know if I'd see Philip again. There was no sign that he was interested in me or that our contact was anything more than polite friendship. So, again, I had to wait and see. I would not chase him but that wait seemed a very long time in coming!

One night, when I couldn't sleep and it was about midnight I felt the Lord ask me to get up and go to my prayer chair in the conservatory. It was dark outside and I sat waiting for the Lord to speak further. He was silent and after a half hour I asked if it was ok to go back to bed. As I rose, I sensed the Lord approach me from behind. I heard Him whisper to my spirit, 'Kathy will you trust me in this one?' I knew He was referring to Philip. I answered immediately, 'Of course, I'll trust you'. It was as though I could feel Him put His hands on my shoulders and say again, 'Kathy will you trust me?' I again answered, but less flippantly, 'Yes, I'll trust you'. It was then as though He turned me around to face Him and said a third time, 'Kathy will you *really* trust me in this!' By this time I was as sober as I could be. I knew that when God spoke three times it was a serious matter, so when I answered again, 'Yes, I will trust you', I knew that things would require me to really hold on to the Lord. I felt the seriousness of His request and I pondered what it could mean. Part of me wondered (as I tried to work out God) if it meant I would be marrying swiftly. As it happened, it was going to be the opposite, a time of waiting patiently through all the twists and turns which followed, which if He hadn't spoken to me might have caused me to walk away from Philip.

**Lesson Learned**
**God only gives such a clear sign when we are really going to need to have to trust Him, somewhere down the road. We need it to hang on to and speak out when the circumstances look contrary.**

Over the coming days I chatted with God about His visit and I was aware of His enjoyment at my excitement. That was so special, to know His involvement in each detail.

I had forgotten what it was like to be in the first flush of a growing love. Not only was it a lovely reminder in the natural but also in the spiritual with my first love for Jesus. As I fell in love with Philip, so it challenged me about reigniting my main love.

I'd forgotten: how you can't get them off your mind; the flutters in the heart area; the adrenalin when the phone rings even though it's unlikely to be him; the ache at being apart; the going over every last intricate detail reliving it; the conversations; the looks; the words; the longing to be back together; the ache to be intimate; the excitement; the desire to tell everyone; the urge to share every little experience with this someone special. In my journal just 6 weeks after we met I wrote:

> *Philip you are always on my mind*
> *in my heart*
> *on my lips*
> *in my heartcry*
> *through my prayers*

As I say, what a poignant reminder of what Jesus means about not losing our first love!

> *How my heart aches*
> *With reawakened love*
> *With yearning for a glimpse*
> *Just a glimpse of your smile*

*Directed at me*
*It lights up my life*
*With a thrill of knowing*
*That I hug secretly*
*To my heart*

My love was awakened, just like the Bible talks about in Song of Songs 2 v7. Philip, though I didn't realise it, was in a totally different place. I'm glad I didn't know because I really enjoyed the whole process of falling in love again and if I'd known where he was actually at, it would have stolen those precious times away from me

As you can see, I'm the romantic, the wordsmith, the heart person. I even listed in my journal all the things (over 40) which were drawing me to Philip – things like his love for the Lord, his smile, enthusiasm, eccentricity. As I read them, I realise I knew him for who he was, very early on in our friendship, for these are the qualities which still draw me to him.

For Philip, however, this journey was far less straight forward!

In the waiting, I began to realise why Jesus had personally come to me to ask me to trust Him completely. It was His words which I would hang onto in the coming months, when my emotions would be untrustworthy and send me all over the place.

I would often have to speak sense to myself, especially when feeling insecure, as my journal shows:

*It's like there's been this cork in my heart, with no outlet for all I have inside to give and to share....what I do need is caution – who I speak to, and how much I share. Also in my mind not to run ahead of myself. I have to remember to trust God and not to try to engineer anything. It's so hard holding back but I must remember Philip's got quite a bit of adjusting to do. He's never been married and might well have put it out of his mind.*

*So, now I must push into God and wait for Him to work it all out!*

As you can see, I was trying to rein in my feelings and not run ahead.

I'm not going to pretend I was very successful in this. I think most of us women, once our hearts get engaged, manage very well to run into the future in our dreams and fantasies. I would really caution against this, as I've seen untold hurt with women who 'believed' way beyond the real circumstances and actually started to live their dreams in a fantasy. It's an important point for women. We need to watch our feelings and be sober in our judgement, even if our emotions are running riot with excitement.

I add this addendum because I've known several lovely women who started to believe fantasies concerning men – even to the point of starting preparations for a wedding without there even being a real relationship. Be careful. Our desires are very strong but must be rooted in reality.

**Lesson Learned**
**It's important to live in the 'now' and the reality of the present, avoiding running ahead in the imagination, which can lead us into heartache unnecessarily.**

And so I waited!

Looking back I see what a short time frame all of this happened in – just the space of 7 weeks, yet it seemed forever. It just shows the intensity of the feelings I was experiencing.

As you can see, I'm the one who is spontaneous, somewhat impatient, knowing my mind. Philip's more the steady, rational, thinking decision maker. How wise of God to put opposites together to balance each other.

Of course, as this new love started to blossom in my heart, I had a further stage of grieving to go through regarding the 'end' of my marriage to Geoff. For a season, there was a tug of war going on in my heart. I realised, with a new relationship birthing there had to be change and for a while I was resistant and there were tears. Part of me didn't want to do that final letting go.

Many people talk of not wanting a 'ghost' in their marriage and I didn't want to do this in my new relationship. So, after a bit of a tussle inside, I decided to take most of Geoff's photos down. More than this, I pulled out my box where all of my treasures associated with Geoff were kept. I proceeded to read all the letters and tear them up. That season had passed. I felt no regret in clearing out, instead, a physical relief, as I moved on to the new phase. I kept the really significant ones and that felt right, an acknowledging of our life together.

I was making room physically but more importantly emotionally, for a new relationship, where I wouldn't be dragged back to the past but instead look to the future.

As I say, this was a very personal walk and I expect other people would deal with a similar situation in their own unique way which might be completely different.

## Lesson Learned
**In order to move into a new relationship, we have to let the past go and make room emotionally and physically for the new. It's a sure sign of whether we're ready for a new relationship, if we can do this. Any resistance might suggest the time's not quite right, or a further stage of healing may be needed, especially if you've had a previous hurt or disappointment that's not been worked through.**

I was continuing to be prayerful and God seemed to be saying 'you have not because you ask not' James 4 v 2. I didn't feel it was a rebuke but an invitation. In response, I prayed that Philip would ring me and ask to meet up whilst he was on holiday that week. Shortly afterwards, he rang to invite me out.

I'm adding the detail because this reveals the intimate leading of the Lord and my need to trust Him. However, before Philip contacted me I went through a real time of battle in my mind and emotions – it was as if the enemy poured cold water over me. I began to doubt the guidance, the friendship and started believing self accusations – who are you to talk about marriage when he hasn't even told you he likes you; you've misinterpreted it all; he's not interested and so the battle of the mind commenced! I still didn't know when I'd see Philip and I was sinking with disappointment – the result of allowing such enthusiasm in my emotions.

God speaks to people in different ways; through the Bible directly, through circumstances; through other people. Yet there are many other ways He's talking, which we can sometimes miss. His creation and the natural world are there for our pleasure. He took great delight in making things beautiful and the Bible tells us that creation points to God, and is a reflection of His glory. In previous centuries, the Celtic saints were known for their interaction with the natural world. I've always had a love of wildlife and the countryside. For me, it's a very natural thing for God to show me something about Himself through things I observe in nature.

One way which God used to specifically encourage me and let me know He was involved was to send me grey herons. These particular birds had a great significance for me because on the way to Geoff's funeral 3 grey herons flew low, right by my car. I knew God had sent them to comfort me. They were exactly the right bird; majestic, beautiful but not flashy or bright. Grey – appropriate. Ever since then, when I needed encouragement, I'd see herons. Well throughout this period, I began to frequently see herons again.

**Lesson Learned**
**Look out for the way God is sending you signs of encouragement. He will send them, but we need to keep our eyes open and recognise them. For us, it was very clearly through birds and rainbows but it will be unique to you and something which He knows will be a blessing to you personally.**

# Is This Our First Official Date?

**A longing fulfilled is a tree of life Prov 13 v 12**

## *Kathy*

Our first official date was memorable when it finally came. We had a wonderful day swimming in the sea, munching lunch companionably, and walking the coastal path. Again it was one of those exquisite Cornish days, full of sunshine and blue seas, where nowhere else in the world compares. Although the day is full of memories, the one which both of us clearly recall, is when a skylark hung in the sky directly above us on the coast path. It was battling to stay in one spot, fighting against a strong wind. It really did seem to be singing praises to God right over our heads! I'm familiar with birds and their behaviour. This was extraordinary, the wind was so strong; it definitely had additional help!

That day was really the beginning. There were enough hints and things said, which let me know Philip certainly wanted to pursue this friendship, 'In God's timing'. I'd find he was talking enthusiastically about things he wanted to share with me back home, or a book he wanted to lend me; and so even though I didn't know when I'd next meet him, at least I knew I would. Did that make it any easier? No! I even wrote in my journal *'I feel I've got big 'L' plates on.'*

From this time on he began to phone me fairly frequently, usually at 10pm for half an hour.

Despite this, there was no mention of a relationship and I went through a serious period of turmoil. Part of this, as you'll read from Philip's account, were the doubts which began to kick in for him and inevitably this had repercussions for me. I kept praying and speaking out truth to myself. *'If Philip's heart needs to change, God can do that. If he needs teaching about wooing me, He can do that too.'* In other words, I knew that God could change the situation and remove obstacles, although ultimately we all have free will and He won't violate that. I also enlisted the prayer support of a few trusted friends – to pray for grace for me, not to pray manipulative prayers for my desired outcome, just to cover us both for the Lord's will to come forth.

This was now the battle time, where the enemy was trying to stop our relationship going forward. Not surprisingly he does take an interest in Christians seeking to marry because he knows we're dangerous to him. I received a prophetic word during this time from some trusted friends who didn't know about Philip. *'I am in a period of travail before the birth and I need to be praying, praising and thanking God so that it doesn't abort. This is a new day.'* Needless to say, I obeyed.

## Lesson Learned
**The enemy hates Christian marriages and will do anything to stop them happening. A favourite ploy is to get us to believe a lie – it might be that we are unlovable, or there are not enough Christians to go round, I'm too old, live in a place with few Christians, I've blown it, I'm too fat, I've missed my chance – you name it, he has a thousand lies ready to feed us, each one specifically designed to hit our own particular weak area. But he can't stop a marriage God is bringing together, unless we believe the lie and give it power to influence our choices.**

The battle was intense and I wasn't aware of how difficult the conflict was getting for Philip internally. I'm a very expressive person and readily touch the arm of another person when enthusiastic about something. However, I noticed with Philip, even with just that simple touch, he would stiffen and involuntarily draw away. I thought perhaps he was ensuring physical purity prior to marriage. I would come to understand what was actually going on, later.

I knew he was on holiday nearby and that we could have met up. Even though he phoned, I realised he had no intention of getting together. I hit a big low and this is how I honestly felt:

*I feel as though I have given him a gift of great price – a beautiful coloured glass faceted ball. It's so fragile and delicate, yet incredibly beautiful. Light dances from it and the colours are iridescent.*

*He took the globe in his hands but then his eyes were pulled off elsewhere
and he dropped the glass globe.*

*It fell and shattered into a 1000 shards, each piercing my heart afresh,
because I entrusted my heart to him – my poor, scarred, broken heart
had begun to beat again with hope – but that was dashed today!'*

The initial bubble of joy had now broken and I was realising we were
in totally different places to each other. I'm prophetic, so much of what
I'd been experiencing was in that realm of 'knowing' about situations,
often ahead of time. Now I was in the period of waiting for this to
materialise in the real world and it was painful. For someone with a
prophetic gifting, the word of the Lord always feels like a 'now' word
and about to be imminently fulfilled. Timing is the hardest thing and
often the hardest area to hear about accurately.

It had taken me great courage to open my heart to love again after
Geoff's death. When you've loved someone deeply and they've been
taken from you abruptly with no 'goodbyes', it can leave scars and pain.
Whilst I knew much of my grief was over, it was still a huge leap of
faith to be willing to love and lose again. Hence I was probably feeling
things a bit more intensely than others might but I was by now
somewhat confused as to what was going on. Without Jesus having
asked me to trust Him, I might have withdrawn at this point, because
of the pain and what I perceived as mixed messages from Philip.

It had been several weeks since I'd seen him and I was beginning to
think I must have misunderstood. Then I arrived home to another
invitation to visit him in Cornwall. He had been putting time aside to
be with God for several days and that's why he hadn't contacted me.
It's amazing how lies and twisted thoughts can come into our minds
and we begin to believe them. When we finally communicated, there
was a rational explanation as to why he hadn't been in touch.

Now things began to get interesting and I was once again in faith for
our relationship. I'd been in my office working that week when I felt
God clearly whisper that Philip was struggling with his sexuality. Well
that explained the odd reaction when we touched. It didn't shock me
but it did make sense and I pondered it a while. When I arrived down

in Cornwall to see him this time, he opened up and shared that he was uncertain about his sexuality. How gracious of God to prepare me, so I wasn't shocked and didn't overreact but had a few days to get used to the situation. We prayed together and I knew he wanted to be free from this confusion. Obviously, it had stopped him marrying, having a family and much more. It also now gave me fuel for prayer and a deeper reliance on God for the timing of this relationship. There was nothing I could do but pray. I couldn't change the situation, neither could Philip. He'd been longing to be free for years and sought counsel and prayer ministry but he was still struggling.

**Lesson Learned**
**I had a choice, either to walk through the seemingly insur-mountable obstacles, believing God's words to me, or to look at the difficulties and give up on the relationship.**

Despite this revelation, we had another gorgeous day. I was blessed by the honesty, transparency and openness of our time together. I realised Philip was sharing these deep issues because he also knew God was up to something and probably drawing us together, therefore they would have to be dealt with. Certainly, the path didn't look straightforward for us and the wisdom of man would say over the coming months, keep well away – but God! What do I mean by that? I mean that God has the final say, not man's wisdom! He tells us not to lean on our own understanding but in all our ways acknowledge Him and He will make our paths straight. (Proverbs 3 v 5,6)

Just as before, on leaving Philip, I didn't know if and when I'd see him again. However, the next day he rang and invited me down to a week long Christian event in Cornwall and to stay at his centre.

That week was a turning point. I ended up staying with Philip and sharing meals and every part of the day with him. We became firm friends and joined in the events with fun and companionship. With loads of others around, I could get to know how he interacted with people, his behaviour, meet his friends, see his passion for Jesus and so much more. Our friendship leapt forward in huge strides – yet, we both knew that God needed to deal with his issues, one step at a time or else it would tear him apart. That caused much frustration for people around us who didn't know the issues he was facing in his sexuality and kept pressuring us to move faster in our relationship. I didn't feel at liberty to share except with my very closest friends, so the pressure of people's teasing, but then obvious frustration with us, was really hard. I'm so glad we worked these things through before we married, took our time and built slowly, carefully at the pace that the Lord led us. By the time we came to marry, there were no secrets, no unexpected surprises and we were best friends.

Well meaning people, family, friends, others all seem to want to have a say in a relationship. In the Christian world especially, we can feel as though we are in a goldfish bowl and opinions are sometimes shared a bit too freely. This can put unnecessary pressure on a couple, especially if you're not in the first flush of youth and there are past issues to be dealt with. It's important at these times to choose your wise counsellors carefully and prayerfully. You want people inputting into your life who are prayerful themselves because most people give their own wisdom, rather than the Lord's and however well meaning it can be totally different from what God is saying.

There is nothing wrong with keeping your relationship somewhat private until you have worked through to a comfortable place together. Having others praying for you, who are for you and have no agenda, is very valuable but again be wise who you ask. Many people don't want change and when we enter a relationship it inevitably changes the balance within friendships and family relationships. Unintentionally, people may want to keep the status quo and this can affect their counsel. Above all, go at your own pace. There really is no hurry. God doesn't deal in pressure, He leads gently. Go at His pace for your relationship and certainly don't take on anyone else's pressure – even the other person in the relationship.

**Lesson Learned**
**Friendship sustains a marriage, long after the initial attraction dims. Overlapping interest and points of mutual enjoyment are really important in the long term. Invest in your friendship.**

So, we'd known each other 4 months, as a long distant relationship. Yet, somehow, we had grown very close but again we were still in different places emotionally. The closer we grew as friends, the more I wanted the normal interaction of a couple. But the closer we grew, the more turmoil was going on internally for Philip. It was really hard for both of us.

**Lesson Learned**
**Pray for your future spouse (whether you've met them yet or not). Pray they will become all that God wants them to be, that they will grow in intimacy with Father God and be prepared by Him for your marriage. Pray for yourself to be the person they will need alongside them and that God would prepare you. Be willing to allow Him to work on you!**

# *Philip*

My journey to the point Kathy is now describing was more tortuous. I was beginning to notice the 'signs' with birds when we were out on walks. I distinctly remember one incident at St Enodoc's church where Sir John Betjeman, the poet, is buried. We sat on a bench in the churchyard and immediately a family of young swallows was flying all around us in circles, swooping in and twittering over us. It was a serenade by birds and it wasn't a fleeting moment but went on the whole time we stayed there. It was so totally out of the normal.

Also, I'd begun to be a bit suspicious that something was happening because twice I was asked if there were a 'Mrs Laity'. The first time was in my bank. I'd been using the same small branch for 20 years and they'd never previously asked. The second time was by an elderly lady who was staying at the Christian centre. I was aware this was God.

Also, whilst Kathy and I were at the Christian event together she mentioned earlier, something surprising happened. On the last evening, whilst everyone was worshipping in song and dance, some friends gathered around us. They held a canopy of silk over our heads, just like in a Jewish marriage ceremony. To me it felt prophetic that God was leading us into marriage. At the time, my 'spirit' knew it was right, whereas my 'soul' was uncomfortable with it.

In the light of the Lord's leading, I arranged to see my vicar, Rev David White (now of St Andrew's Chorleywood) for a bit of wise counsel, hoping he would speak sense into me, that I was imagining what was going on. I think I wanted him to tell me that I was being silly and to go home and forget the whole idea. He listened. We prayed together and he had a verse of scripture come to mind:

*See! The winter is past;*
*The rains are over and gone.*
*Flowers appear on the earth;*
*The season of singing has come,*
*The cooing of doves*
*Is heard in our land*
*The fig-tree forms its early fruits;*
*The blossoming vines spread their fragrance.*
*Arise come my darling*
*My beautiful one, come with me.*
*Song of Solomon 2 v 11-13*

It wasn't really the verse I wanted to hear; taken from the love book of the Bible, all about birds singing over us and spring coming. Yet, I knew he had heard God and that God was speaking to me.

So, I went home and I had a few words with God. Basically my prayer was 'You wouldn't ever ask someone to get married who doesn't want to and is happy single, would you?' I did a thing I don't really recommend for usual guidance but I took my Bible and let it open at random. It opened to Hosea 1 v 2 'Go take to yourself an adulteress wife.' Here was God asking one of his children to marry someone he clearly wouldn't have naturally wanted to marry. I think this is the only point in the Bible where God does command someone to marry, hence He took me to that verse. That had been my question and He had answered. My reaction was to quickly shut the Bible and put it down and ignore what I'd just read!

Soon after this, I was asking the question again. 'Surely you wouldn't tell someone to marry who really does not want to?' I took a different Bible, just to be on the safe side, and randomly opened it again – to the same verse! Oh boy, I couldn't deny that God was speaking. If this had been the only guidance I wouldn't have taken it, obviously, but in the light of all that had been happening, with the signs with birds (and rainbows) on our walks, the growing sense of God up to something and the counsel of my vicar, I was now faced with a dilemma. God seemed to want this of me – but still I didn't want it. Yet, because of this clear guidance, a confidence began to build in me that what God asks of one of His children, He provides the Grace to fulfil it. It wasn't an overnight change, but I knew God was faithful. He would make the way.

# God, What's Going On?

**Plans fail for lack of counsel, but with many advisors they succeed.**
**Prov 15 v 22**

## *Kathy*

In a normal relationship, there's usually a linear progression. You get to know each other step by step, each step taking you closer together. I think that was my perception anyway.

How different was the one I found myself in. Contrasting with the early days soon after I'd met Philip, when I was full of joy and anticipation, trusting God to move us swiftly together; I now found myself in the slough of despond, with little in the natural to hold on to. The more I felt for Philip, the more turmoil he experienced because of the confusion in his sexuality. It became an agonising time for both of us.

However, despite the difficulties, one day as we talked together, he acknowledged that we were a couple, and that God was doing something between us! We had spent the day walking around Tintagel and experienced two more amazing signs from God. We called into a chapel on the coast path near Tintagel. A family of baby swallows were nesting in the porch, twittering right over us. Then when we re-entered Tintagel village, there was a spectacular rainbow spanning the main street, so bright and breathtaking that it made us stop in our tracks.

It felt like God was shouting His encouragement to us with such beautiful encounters with His creation. We had admitted that we were now a couple but for Philip he said it's the scariest thing and biggest step of faith he's ever made.

Just a day after this time with Philip I was back home alone and had the most extraordinary experience. Looking back, I can see that every time I had a really unusual spiritual encounter, it was to strengthen me for what lay ahead.

One night, I was woken by the sound of angel wings and singing! I made myself wake up fully, to check it wasn't the dawn chorus of birds, but no, it was 1am and no birds were singing. I felt renewed hope and joy spring up inside me, ready for what lay ahead!

The next month was spent in Cornwall, running my business from a rented cottage. I felt it was important that I was nearer, so that Philip and I could spend some more normal time together and that meant putting myself out a bit.

Philip at this time told me he would like me as his wife – *if* God set him free. He loved my company, felt at ease with me *but* was not in love with me. He knew that part of his heart was missing, closed down and not functioning. He loved me as much as he was able to love anyone

Wow! No-one wants to hear that the man they are being called to marry doesn't love them! I didn't want someone to marry me on obedience, without love......It must have been God's grace which buoyed me up, because I could have been devastated at this point, yet I wasn't.

Despite these times of private honesty and turmoil, we found ourselves beginning to minister together occasionally at the regular healing meetings he held at his centre and we began to meet the significant people in each other's lives.

There were also very light-hearted moments, where glimpses of our future freedom together manifested. I remember us both swinging on a rope over the River Fowey, laughing and feeling exuberant. It was so appealing and so normal and these moments gave me hope to continue!

About this time, God also starting speaking to me from Song of Songs saying the 'winter is past and the rains have gone. The season of singing is here.' (The same scripture which Philip's vicar had felt the Lord speaking for him). It goes on to talk about the cooing of turtle doves is heard in the land. These verses began to pop up more and more, whilst circumstances started to go in the opposite direction again.

However, more trials followed and the weekend Philip met my mum and her husband was particularly trying. Obviously the relationship was becoming more real and the pressure on his sexuality and decisions was causing a huge amount of inner turmoil. At this point God had not set him free and it was agony for him. This showed in anxiety and exhaustion, so he wasn't able to fully participate in the weekend. After my mum had left we inevitably talked. By then, I was churned up emotionally and feeling fairly wretched.

Philip's way of coping was to withdraw and become quite remote from me. However, he owned up to being emotionally mixed up and scared. We were finding it hard being in the public gaze without people knowing the full reasons behind us taking things slowly. Also, we were both aware we actually needed a miracle for us to ever be able to progress. No wonder God came to me so early on and asked me to trust Him. I had no idea what He was asking of me! I wrote the following heart cry when my eyes were on the difficulties of what we were facing:

*So close*
*With a fissure between us*
*As deep and fathomless as any divide*
*Yet I reach across*
*With hands outstretched to yours meeting mine*
*The longing*
*To jump*
*Prematurely across the chasm...*
*WAIT*

*I hear the cry*
*Look up and remember*
*I cannot jump to your side*
*Nor you to mine*
*The fissure as deep as any high*
*Mountain*
*Must fuse and be healed*
*Before we can move towards*
*each other*
*And stand face to face on the ground*
*Where once it was.*
*Whole, together*
*At last!*

In the natural, I was crying out for someone to love me and not just be obedient to God. Though we loved each other's company, it was not enough. I wrote in my journal:

*We need miracles. Neither of us can change our circumstances or his health and wholeness. It's a trust issue. Will I trust God to do it?*

*Then I turned on God TV and Rick Joyner was saying at that moment, 'Trust is the bridge over the chasm. The stronger the trust, the greater the load it can bear'.*

*I trust Philip and I trust God. So what if there's a chasm, I can now look at the bridge of trust to get me through.*

Why am I sharing the convoluted twists and turns of our relationship – because I think many people need to hear an honest account? Often with testimonies we hear of the spiritual highs and the wonderful experiences but the lows are not recorded and it can give a distorted view of reality. I'm hoping that by us being brutally honest many people will come into freedom to marry. To help others, is our main reason for recording so openly before our readers and it wouldn't be truthful if I only talked about the visit of Jesus, or the angels and the high points without also revealing the lows and the hindrances.

What I did begin to notice was how God responded to my desperation and honesty. When I tried to hold it together, be the strong 'Christian' I often found myself struggling but if I went before God in total honesty things happened. For instance there was one day when I was convinced there was little future to any of it!

I seemed to have fallen into a wallow of self-pity which is not attractive; some of it was looking at the circumstances and saying they were the truth, rather than what God had said; easy to say in hindsight, but hard to know at the time. So this is what I recorded in my journal:

*Everything and everyone else gets priority.....but it's not sour grapes, it's the disappointment....I never know when I'm going to see him next.*

*I never know if he wants me to ring. I feel a nuisance being around, an inconvenience, an embarrassment .....I'm walking on eggshells....I don't think I can stand this pressure any longer – well I couldn't tonight. I feel so alone in it....This is the most abnormal relationship.*

An interesting aside here and one which I think we women need to learn: I was correctly noticing his behaviour i.e. in avoiding me, getting ultra busy but I was totally wrong in my assumptions and conclusions i.e. that I was a nuisance, an embarrassment etc; that was my own insecurity speaking. In fact, these were his avoidance techniques because he was also insecure and in turmoil emotionally.

So, my reaction was to leave a meeting early and go back home. I was pretty upset. *It's as though he's almost willing the relationship not to work, as if he's convinced it's not going to. All my joy and expectation is disappearing.*

I was in an emotional mess. I was confused. I was trying to work it out myself, trying to trust God, trying to trust Philip. But it was hard and that night I hit a particular low. I listened to the lies and sadly started agreeing with them.

*I genuinely felt like leaving and going back to Devon. Have I got this totally wrong? If God hadn't spoken so clearly in those early days, I probably wouldn't still be around.*

Can you hear the familiar ring of the enemy's taunts? 'Did God really say this?' Just like he tempted Adam and Eve right back in the beginning, he was tempting me now to doubt God's word to me.

Just like David in some of his psalms, I vented my emotion and then got a clearer perspective.

*I know in my pain, I'll be exaggerating. I also know clearly God was leading us together. However, it takes the wills of two people.*

I wanted to be the most important person in his life and I was impatient. I don't blame myself but I can see how some of the pain was self inflicted. There's a wise Bible verse in Song of Songs 8 v 4, which tells us not to awaken love before its time. Perhaps I allowed my heart to fully open to love ahead of time.

Anyway, I vented my frustration and all the other angst to God that night, with tears and honesty.

What a difference a day makes!

The morning came and I was refreshed and looking at things far more clearly. I knew I needed to talk directly with Philip. Just as I set out to find him, he was driving to me and we met half way.

That day I shared my disappointments and struggles. He listened. I'm not sure he understood but he heard me out. He had also gone to the trouble of putting brunch together, bringing me roses and being attentive in many little ways. He must have known I was struggling.

The thing which blessed me was that God knew my needs as well as Philip's. It was all very well me having to hang on, wait etc but I did have legitimate needs which were now coming to the surface. God impressed on Philip that I needed his time that day and it happened.

**Lesson Learned**
**I'm convinced some of these interactions happened because God was invited right into our courtship. We were both praying every step of the way, therefore when I poured my heart out to God crying for some forward movement, because Philip was also prayerful and open to God, he could be led by the Holy Spirit to come alongside me in the ways I needed. Neither of our needs was right or wrong, just different.**

One of the things which we weren't really doing very well, was being honest with ourselves. I was beginning to lose my self respect, just waiting for Philip to call or not call, invite me down to Cornwall or ignore me for a week or so. Even though I was running my own business, had my own circle of friends and church, I began to put my life on hold, waiting for his decisions. As a result, without realising it, I was beginning to feel some resentment and move into a less than healthy way of relating, where all my boundaries were being trashed and allowing myself to be controlled by him. He wasn't deliberately doing this, understand, but it was the resultant effect of me not stating clearly my own needs for clear communication about when and how we would meet. I allowed his turmoil to dictate all the decisions.

It came to a head one evening in my church fellowship, when I suddenly seemed to see clearly what I was allowing. I was so upset, I left the meeting and when my two friends found me, we talked long and hard. The upshot was that I decided to draw back from the relationship until Philip was more sorted and able to commit properly to our future. I felt fear as I realised I was going to make this decision but also relief. The fear came from knowing that he might never change and therefore I would lose him, but in one sense I never 'had' him. However, the friendship was now a significant one for me and I cherished it. The relief came from knowing that I was no longer going to be at his beck and call. I needed to reassert some good boundaries, about self respect and having my own life back.

**Lesson Learned**
**In the midst of wanting to be married, don't lose your self –respect or allow behaviour which violates your personal boundaries. There's no need to be that desperate and it also sets a precedent which can be unhealthy later on in the relationship.**

I wrote him a long letter ending our relationship until he could say he truly wanted it to happen and posted it. Interestingly, the letter never arrived! To this day we have no idea where it ended up.

Some days later he invited me down to visit. I decided to see him, so we could talk things through face to face.

## *Philip*

I invited Kathy down for a day. I wrote in my journal:

> *We had good chats about how we were both feeling. Kathy found it so hard the way I saw her at my convenience and dropped her when I wanted. She wants an ongoing relationship, not fits and starts. I shared*

*some of the scriptures God was giving me and extracts from the marriage book I was reading.*

We continued to have signs when together and on that day saw a rainbow and then most extraordinarily a peacock. This was particularly relevant for me, as I'd received a prophetic word years previously that God was changing me from being like a chicken into a peacock. It crossed the road right in front of us, down a small Cornish lane!

# Kathy

It turned out to be a delightful time, away from others' eyes and once again it was a joy to be together. We talked, I learned to communicate my needs and he listened. All the struggles just seem to wash away again.

**Lesson Learned**
**I've noticed in other situations with people; the enemy builds a lie in our minds which a meeting face-to-face dispels and blows effortlessly away.**

With this privacy Philip and I were able to make some forward steps. We spent many days together, as I was still renting the cottage in Cornwall, and could pop over more easily. Looking back it's quite surreal because once the communication doors were open nothing seemed to be off limits. We talked about previous relationships, marriage, sex, friendship, our feelings for each other and what it would be like to be married! I saw so much forward movement in Philip that I hung on in with the relationship. He now admitted feelings for me were beginning and he shared guidance God had already given him about me i.e. that I would be his 'Ruth'. For me this was significant, because of God telling me I'd marry a 'Boaz'.

My journal is packed full of God's words of encouragement and promptings to trust Him, plus strategies on how He wanted me to pray.

*He will come free, in My time, in My way – but you must continue to trust me. Don't try to force anything when it seems too hard, see My eyes of love twinkling at you. For I see the end from the beginning. I see your marriage, a marriage made in heaven, a marriage which will be a torch which many others will follow and be drawn to.*

I obviously needed to be told to trust again and again and again.

**Lesson Learned**
**Interestingly, God's 'now' or 'soon' are very different from mine and these words came very shortly before another crisis happened. As always, God wanted me to have His perspective beforehand, so that I could choose to believe Him and not what circumstances were presenting.**

There had been strides forward but I was still puzzled. Philip had clear guidance from God, was sharing deeply, talking about marriage and moving towards me physically, even saying he thought many of his fears would fall way when we were married – yet he held back. I was expecting something to become clearer for him but it didn't seem to.

# Philip

Whilst Kathy was down in Cornwall for that month, I was continually seeking God and recording His responses to me in my journal. His patient hand was always encouraging me.

*28/11/04: There is much ahead for you and Kathy, so do not linger My son. Philip I am pleased with you and delight in you the way you are proceeding. I know it's not been easy but as you remain faithful to me, My grace will empower you for all that's ahead.*

*3/12/04: I was reading an outstanding and beautifully written book on marriage and found the following extract really helpful.*

*'If a couple were to seek the Lord with their whole will, rejoice in Christian fellowship and spend time both alone and together in heartfelt prayer and study of scriptures, they would soon find their love life filled with a rich glow and a mysterious new energy which cannot be discovered through any worldly means'. The Mystery of Marriage by Mike Mason P155/156*

As you can see from these entries, God was encouraging me in my prayer and journaling times, with words from scripture, books I was reading, signs in nature and words coming from other people. He was building a picture of reassurance and encouragement, which I couldn't just ignore.

## Kathy

I'd now spent a month in Cornwall and things appeared to be moving forward. But then Philip hit a full blown crisis which I didn't see coming. When we'd been alone we'd had a fabulous time. The tension seemed to come when other people were around.

One weekend, back at my Devon home, Philip and some friends were staying. He hadn't slept for two nights and was really churned up. Our friend warned me he was about to break up with me.

*I went into shock. I felt it hit me and resonate through my body. I collapsed in tears – just crumpled. The enormity of the situation hit me. Everything went through my head – all that God has said and done. I know our relationship is of Him!*

*Yet whilst prostrate on the floor, out of my mouth came my heart cry. I am Yours Lord, only Yours. Have Your way.*

There's only been one other time in my life when I've been tested to the limit like this and that was when the policeman told me that Geoff had been killed. Both times my heart's cry was for Jesus; nothing else but Him. When you've been to the bottom and looked at the worst that life and the enemy can throw at you and realise that Jesus is ingrained in your innermost being, it's hugely reassuring. Why? Because He promises never to let me go and not to test me beyond what I can bear. He never lies and His promises are true.

Nevertheless, it took me a huge amount of courage to walk into the lounge, knowing Philip was going to walk away from me. He looked ill and tired. He was traumatised by our relationship, fearful of having a breakdown. Our miracle just hadn't happened yet!

Initially I thought he was totally ending our relationship. He'd done this to someone else about 8 years previously, so I asked him to spell out exactly what was happening because he mustn't ever put another woman through what he'd put her, and now me!

He'd received counsel the night before that said, if he didn't have peace after prayer then he should 'step out of the situation with me.' He didn't have peace and because he trusted this friend, he stepped away from me.

I double checked whether he was ending it with me but he said 'no' because he could see all the signs God had given us. He just needed time to spend with God and get counselling ministry.

Despite writing to break it off myself a month previously, when he did it, I was devastated. It was now December, just before Christmas, we'd met on the 1st May and nothing seemed to have changed. Plus my closest friend was leaving and moving up country in just 4 weeks. I literally felt as if my life was falling apart. We did talk about a way forward but it was agreed that I wouldn't contact him, except occasionally writing. He 'might' be in touch from time to time. He was going to prioritise getting prayer ministry.

## Philip

It was crisis time. We'd been spending some lovely days together, growing close and were firm friends but as we drew nearer the inner turmoil increased, as well as the spiritual battle opposing our marriage. I went into a full blown anxiety state and I knew that if I didn't take the pressure off I could have a breakdown. It was a totally involuntary emotional meltdown, where I was churned up internally, not sleeping and suffering physically. I was traumatised in my emotions, body, mind and will. I was in freefall and did the only thing I thought I could do, I withdrew from Kathy. At a church meeting the previous night I sought counsel from an old and wise Christian friend who'd known me many years. He said 'I needed some space, in view of how I was feeling'.

Thankfully, Kathy let me go without trying to control the situation, releasing me to seek healing and make my own decisions. I know it hurt her immeasurably and we have had to work that through but both of us can honestly say there are now no shadows left from those days.

Basically what was happening with me, were all the fears of marriage I'd ever had were surfacing.

It was simpler to withdraw and try to contain what was coming up rather than face my emotional baggage. I could no longer hide behind this mask but had to be real. Now aware that I was shut down emotionally, I was also battling some very selfish motives. I didn't want to lose my independence and become inter dependent with another person. Also, I wasn't convinced I had what it took to be a husband sexually, or that my body was in the least bit attractive physically. For a while I believed the lies the enemy fed me and which I turned round in my logical mind.

Yet, after just a few days the anxiety settled down but then I defaulted to my usual way of coping, I involved myself busily in doing things, so I still wouldn't have to face these issues. We are all very adept at building coping mechanisms and mine was to compartmentalise my life, listen to the logic of what I'd done and not really think at all of the fall out for Kathy. It's not a good admission but I literally didn't realise the anguish I was putting her through. I was so self absorbed in my own pain.

However, God's grace intervened and gradually, step by step the journey continued. As my journal entries show I was still prayerful about our relationship.

*23/12/04: Asked God for scripture re Kathy and was led again to Hosea, this time Ch 3 where Hosea was asked by the Lord to show his love to his wife again.*

*30/12/04: An elderly friend of mine shared how her daughter refused to marry a man, but then many years later God told her to marry him, even though she wasn't in love. The marriage has turned out to be especially blessed. In such circumstances she said that if God was in it, I should make the jump.*

Interestingly, some time later, two friends spoke to me the same words, 'Philip, it's time for you to jump through the hoop!' With the help of those words, I found the courage to move forward gently again and thankfully Kathy waited and forgave me.

# Kathy

He left, with no promise of ever being in touch again. I had to choose how to respond. Would I sink into self pity or rise up in faith, hanging on to the words and scriptures God had given me over so many months. I chose the latter and declared war in the heavenlies in prayer.

I had already been robbed of one husband and I knew that I knew God had spoken, so I went into praise and refused to come into agreement this time, with the negative thoughts and emotions. I chose to agree with the promises God had given me. I resolved in my heart to praise, to worship, to declare the Biblical promises I had regarding this marriage and to stand.

Though my emotions felt shot to pieces and there was a physical ache in my heart, I was determined. I knew God as faithful. I went on a fast eating only fruit and vegetables for several weeks. This was not to manipulate Philip, but to seek God and stand with Philip in his desire for freedom. In my journal I wrote:

*This seems the toughest path God has asked me to walk along for a long, long time. I'm scared I'll be weak and fail, not cope on my own especially my friend moving as well and Christmas coming but with God I can do all things. Yet I will praise Him.*

I wrote out scriptures God had been giving me concerning this relationship and ones He'd given over my life. I wrote out warfare scriptures, really contesting with the enemy for this man's freedom. I also enlisted the prayer support of trusted friends.

**Lesson Learned**
**A week before Christmas I had a beautiful revelation of a little of what God was up to in the midst of all this. He always seems to have a wider perspective and just as I'd been aware of rekindling my first love for Jesus, when I was falling in love with Philip, now He showed me a revelation of His suffering. He showed me I was sharing what He suffers over everyone who turns away from Him. He's lovesick, hurting, aching, thinking of them continually. He loves them passionately but so many just turn their backs on Him. It breaks His heart.**

Nevertheless, these days seemed endless, the reality began to hit, and I didn't know if this separation would be days, weeks or months. I still chose to look by faith and not by sight as otherwise, I could sink into hopelessness and despair. I spent much time in prayer walking, praising, intimate worship, declaration and warfare. I fasted in the end for 17 days, finishing at Christmas.

In the natural there seemed little change and I couldn't even say I'd felt a breakthrough in the spiritual, so I just had to stand. I didn't believe God was setting me up for heartbreak. He'd told me to trust Him. I knew Philip's integrity and that he knew God was drawing us to marriage, so I had to wait and trust. I had to continually choose not to harden my heart to him and to forgive where he'd hurt me.

And still God gave me signs. On Christmas Eve when I was a bit morose, having expected to spend Christmas with Philip, I woke at 2am and 3am, to hear a robin singing outside my bedroom window.

Philip did ring me on Christmas day and then a week later popped in unexpectedly but we were strained and polite. However, I commented that his face looked different, somehow lighter. His answer encouraged me. He said he knew an enemy assignment had left him that morning. I praised God. Could this be fruit of my fasting and prayer, a glimmer of hope?

# Philip

I continued to seek God regarding Kathy and marriage, even though I'd drawn back from actively pursuing the relationship. My journal is full of my entreaties before God.

*Out of the blue, another person, asked if I was married. Prior to my courtship with Kathy, I don't recall ever being asked this question. It was as if God was provoking me to think about marriage.*

# Kathy

At the same time as being refined by God in my relationship, I was also facing severe pressures in my business. At the beginning of the new year my back was against the wall. *My prayer at this time was Lord I will do what I can, please do what I can't.* This prayer seemed to crack open the favour of God and work started to come in again and new opportunities opened up. The Bible verse I was clinging to was 'Trust (lean on, rely on) in the Lord with all your heart and lean not on your own understanding. In all your ways acknowledge Him and He will direct your path.' Proverbs 3 v 5,6 (Amp)

And with the beginning of the new year, came the move of my closest friend . We had been used to living in each other's pockets and she had been the closest when helping me through Geoff's death. At the time she said 'I'm here for the long haul!' and she was faithful to her word. Now, she was relocating with work to the other side of the country. It was a real wrench for both of us, yet we knew God's hand was in it.

With all that was happening with this friend and my business, thankfully my mind was no longer preoccupied with Philip. Part of me was still deeply shocked and hurt by his behaviour and I was guarding my heart carefully.

However, the day after my friend moved in January, Philip contacted me unexpectedly after several weeks interval and we spent the day together. I didn't think it was coincidental but God manoeuvred. We met half way between his home and mine, which was on Dartmoor. We climbed a tor (a rocky outcrop unique to Dartmoor), a huge rainbow spanned our way, set against perfectly blue sky. We took things gently. He asked forgiveness for badly hurting me and so our relationship once more started moving forward.

## Lesson Learned

I had to choose to let go of the hurt and pain Philip had caused me and trust him again. I had to look beyond the circumstances, to the person I knew him to be in God; someone kind, Godly, committed to working things out. If I hadn't forgiven him fully, I think the relationship would have been tainted and bitterness would have grown at the centre of it, which probably would have killed it. The Apostle Paul says love 'does not keep a record of wrongs' 1 Cor 13 v 5.

# Are We Stuck? A Season of Contending

**He hears the prayer of the righteous. Prov 15 v 29**

## *Kathy*

The early weeks of 2005 continued to be difficult. Although Philip was in touch, we were not meeting privately, just at church events and conferences, with a few hours chatting afterwards. I was aware the intimacy we had shared was gone. The openness wasn't there and I was cautious, feeling my way and wondering where I stood.

However, since Philip had backed away in early December, I was having very intimate times with the Lord. He was wooing me to press in deeper to Him, in much more meaningful ways. I was learning more about His intense love for me, His passionate jealousy for my life and His desire to spend time with me and share His heart. I wouldn't have missed this for the world. So, even though my way forward with Philip was strained, there was a real time of growth with God and a hunger for Him like I've rarely experienced. I was living the truth of, 'if we draw near to Him, He draws near to us' (James 4:8) and He is 'a rewarder of those who diligently seek Him.' (Hebrews 11:6). I literally couldn't function without Him.

During this time we were introduced by some friends to Andrew and Carole Baker, over a meal. We'd not met them before and they didn't know our situation. Both of them are moving accurately in the prophetic. Part way through the meal, Carole started to cry and take off a beautiful green gemmed ring which she was wearing. She told me the Lord had asked her to give it to me. I was a bit embarrassed and asked her why? She turned round to look at a wedding photo on the dresser behind her, where the wedding ring was very prominent and I knew it was as if I were being given an engagement ring. As she did this, Andrew then started to prophesy over us both. There was a lot to the prophecy but what's relevant to this book I've included below:

*"God makes everything beautiful in its time. ...Calling forth life, preparing for a wife...This is what I want to do for you both. It will be a beautiful thing. That's why the ring!"*

I sensed Philip was squirming beside me and I didn't really know how to respond. I put the ring on the ring finger of my right hand, actually wondering if this would be my engagement ring. I ended up wearing it there rather longer than anticipated. It was God's way of encouraging me to hang on, whilst I was waiting for Philip's proposal. He was saying, this relationship is of Me!

# Philip

The day before Carole gave Kathy the ring, I'd met with a close friend for a walk. He was a brother whose wisdom and counsel I trusted and sought out. I shared with him what was happening with Kathy, knowing God was preparing my heart for the way forward. He felt there was a little boy within that needed to be recognised and given permission to surface.

*I need to get in touch with emotions and feelings. I've been trying to crucify part of me that needs to come to life.*

*Isaiah 43 v18-20: Forget the former things, do not dwell on the past. See, I am doing a new thing! Now it springs up, do you not perceive it? I am making a way in the desert and streams in the wasteland.*

Rereading my journal entries, I realise God was gently nudging me forward.

*I spoke to a trusted friend today. Two to three weeks ago, he felt the Lord say 'tie the knot'. He's had it twice now for me. Since then he's prayed further and has felt even more sure it is right for us to marry. He was the one who knew a little boy was trapped within me who is believing*

*Satan's lie that I've not got what it takes to be a man. I have a wound which only God can heal but as I face the fears they will melt away.*

I seemed to need constant reassurance at this time to walk through and face my fears.

# Kathy

In April I returned to writing more personally in my journal:

*All this year we have been gradually, at a snail's pace, moving closer – but I was only seeing him in church meetings and never privately. Eventually I wrote to him saying I needed him to open his heart to me. He's beginning to do this more.*

The outcome was I again went down to Cornwall, the first time in 4 months. We now arranged to go to the Isles of Scilly together. I was taken aback, that he suggested this after the apparent distancing. I was also pleased. It would allow us time to get to know each other without being in the scrutiny of others' gaze and it would be fun!

We stayed in a guesthouse overlooking the main bay on St Mary's the largest island in the Isles of Scilly. We'd been given single rooms at the back of the guest house but the view from the guest lounge was awesome and definitely made up for the lack of view from our rooms. This was a totally different experience for both of us. We were out of our own comfort zones. We were here, as a couple and it took some adjusting for both of us. On the first day I was very insecure picking up on how uncomfortable Philip still was. We had now known each other a year but I was still facing the 'push me-pull me' situation of his healing journey.

However, once we started exploring the islands together we naturally slipped back into our friendship, where shared interests overlapped and brought common ground.

**Lesson Learned**
**It had taken five months for Philip to really find his way back**
**towards me and in that time it would seem that God broke both of**
**us, forging us into new vessels. It was painful, at times excruciating**
**but there was purpose in it and hope along the way. Patience was**
**being grafted into me and faith for what seems impossible.**

However, despite everything, we were stuck. Philip was still acting on
obedience rather than love. He still hadn't come into full freedom but
he did long for the normality of marriage and all that goes with it. He
was committed to seeing this through.

At that point we were really wondering whether God wanted us to
'go ahead anyway', in faith and get married but neither of us wanted
to make such a huge step without confirmation. It could be a recipe
for immense hurt. We did not act, but waited.

# Philip

*16th May 2005*
I prayed this prayer, recording it in my journal.

> *Dear Lord, I believe my anxiety/heart condition is now due to my lack*
> *of decision. I hereby today make a decision to proceed and marry*
> *Katherine and trust you to lift the fears/anxiety off me in Jesus' name*
> *and to release feelings for her.*

(Kathy's aside: This date was 5 years to the day that Geoff was killed –
16th May 2000! Philip didn't know this. I didn't know this until we came
to write this book. How amazing is God. Five is the number of Grace.
God is in the tiniest details.)

# Kathy

Despite all God was saying to Philip, he still couldn't seem to act and by now I was sinking. At the end of June, I decided to go away for the summer and remove myself from the situation totally, to get some clarity, give Philip space and seek God for what was next. Before I went, I spent 3 days with Philip down in Cornwall, a good time, a time once more where we drew closer and talked honestly and then I was gone, up to Shropshire for a couple of months.

I took my business and relocated up to my friend's new home. I plugged in at her church, with her new friends and settled into a rhythm of working from her home. In the midst of the confusion I was feeling, I determined to remain thankful. I made long lists of things I could thank God for, to counteract the continual bombardment which was trying to make life look hopeless and which was constantly undermining what God had said.

# Philip

If the Lord sees that we can be more effective for Him with a spouse than without, he'll bring us the right companion in his perfect time. By surrendering the right to be married, we can be confident that our marital status is fixed in the centre of God's will. Even after going to a leadership school at Toronto Airport Fellowship, things were still not straightforward and I was frequently before the Lord asking for help. Around this time, I went to Lin Button's ministry, one with a real heart to help those with gender issues. In my journal I wrote:

*Dear Lord, well here I am on my 4th day, receiving brilliant teaching by Lin Button but still awaiting a breakthrough. I do trust you but would appreciate encouragement especially after yesterday's ministry with a counsellor from their ministry team, who inferred I shouldn't marry unless I'm in love. She said if the feelings aren't there before marrying they won't be afterwards!*

I sensed God's response was as follows:

*Philip, my son, I know how you're feeling! Philip the days are moving forward, like a train on tracks and things will come to pass as I determine. Your job is to keep going. Trust me to work in your heart and bring you into freedom. Son I understand.*

My heart felt prayers were being heard by God and He would address the specific fears, or lies I was believing, such as the one that I wasn't loveable.

**Lesson Learned**
**During the ministry I did come to an understanding of why I was as I was. The lack of self acceptance and the unhealed parts of me were trying to find wholeness by looking at other men. This was the main root problem. I needed now to accept myself and how God has made me and ask the Father to affirm my manhood. I asked Jesus into all the childhood traumas.**

On the last day of the conference, after the communion service, a couple sang 'God has changed your name'. I sensed the Holy Spirit coming on me very strongly especially during the words 'your new name will be overcoming one'. It felt more significant than anything that had happened throughout the whole time and brought great hope to my heart.

I decided to fast for a few days on returning from the ministry, really seeking God again for more help. I was staying in Kathy's home in Devon for a break, whilst she was in Shropshire.

*Father, as much as I appreciate the signs in nature, the prophecies and the scriptures, I would appreciate something more direct to bring assurance. However, as I know that faith and risk go together I expect at the end of the day I may have to jump!*

*Philip, I have heard your prayer and already I am on your case. Things will happen that will astound you so trust Me and expect good things.*

*Philip you are a special son of Mine and My favour is all over you.*

Even though God was speaking so clearly and I laugh now at how much reassurance I needed, I suppose I wanted something even more striking because inside I didn't feel the issues were dealt with!

I again sought out wise counsel from some friends and Kathy's vicar. All of them seemed to say that it didn't seem wise to proceed into marriage when the feelings weren't there. I was confused. On the one hand there was God giving me all this leading but on the other, the counsel of man (people I respected) was saying don't proceed.

**Lesson Learned**

**I learned from these encounters that counsel is not always from God but can be coming from a person's own thoughts, and their advice is coloured by their own experiences. We need to ensure we are giving and receiving God's counsel for any situation, irrespective of our own thoughts on the matter.**

**The point is, on such an important issue, people should seek God to hear what He is saying, before giving counsel. The walk of faith doesn't always look like the right thing to do! God does tell us not to lean on our own understanding but often this is just what we do.**

The next day, I went for a walk up a local hill with a beacon on the top. I was continuing to pray for encouragement concerning Kathy and was led to Romans 7 v3: 'If a woman's husband dies, she is free to remarry'. This seemed especially apt to our situation.

I also prayed to see a pair of birds, as God so often spoke through birds to us. I'd been seeing single birds but not a pair since staying at Kathy's home. I walked to the top of the beacon and sat down on a wooden bench in the sun. I looked up and saw a pair of buzzards flying directly over my head!

**Lesson Learned**

**Keep exercising faith, even when desperate and continually seek to hear God personally. He'll tell you if you've veered off path.**

Before leaving to return to Cornwall, Kathy returned to her home and we walked up the beacon together. At the top by the wooden bench, where I'd previously prayed to see a pair of birds, we saw two white doves fly passed as we sat in the sun.

One thing I find interesting, when rereading my journals of this time, is that I made a big omission. Throughout my stay at Kathy's, whilst she was in Shropshire, I was attending her village parish church. I used to go to the mid-week communion service and afterwards I walk around the church imagining myself getting married there! On occasions, I used to pray for our wedding day, for fine weather and for God's blessing on the whole service. At this point, it would seem that my *spirit* was ahead of my *soul*, because at the time, I still couldn't cope with going through with the marriage.

We again went our separate ways, I back to Cornwall and Kathy stayed in Devon. We would meet up socially and talk by phone but still we were at a distance. Then in late October, things suddenly began to change. God sent me a clear message again through Andrew Baker, the prophet who had prophesied our marriage when his wife gave Kathy her ring.

He came and gave me two words. '*Get married!*' He had been shown by God that when a couple come together who are yielded to God and to one another, the anointing is greatly multiplied and Satan hates it. Hence the severe spiritual opposition I was experiencing.

Between the end of October and the end of November God started to speak really clearly and frequently. I was led to Proverbs 12v4 'A wife of noble character is a husband's crown.' Another friend who knew us both said he felt we ought to get together soon.

Then I met up with a friend at the end of November who I'd seen many months ago in relation to Kathy. He was a wise mentor to me and he was reminded of the word God had given him: 'Tie the knot'.

Another person said he felt '*there was a decision that I needed to make but was postponing.*' He felt I was too concerned with what people think.

At the end of November I spent a lovely weekend with Kathy and it was so restful and enjoyable. Whilst there, I again enquired of the Lord.

*Lord, is there anything You want to say about Kathy?*

*Philip, My son, the plans I have for you depend on you taking the next step to move forward My child.*

**Lesson Learned**

By trusting God and continually seeking Him, when the time came to act, He was no longer saying 'step by step' but clearly speaking for me to move forward. There was no confusion. For a while He spoke and allowed me to procrastinate but then when I was still holding back, He began to speak more firmly. He obviously knew Kathy would walk away and that there was now a time limit.

The next weekend we also spent together, 2-3 December.

*Kathy had prepared a lovely candlelit meal for us both. We shared communion together around the table and prayed. Kathy poured her heart out to the Lord and we prayed together. Sensed a strong presence of God. I 'saw' a ring and a veil come down from above. I felt/sensed I should now make a proposal of marriage but still held back out of fear.*

*Following this, I couldn't sleep all night. Felt troubled in my heart. Perhaps my disobedience? I asked for a scripture and was led to Saul. He became troubled because of his disobedience. 'To obey is better than sacrifice'.*

The next day I really sought the Lord again and He was by now speaking very clearly.

*Yes, My son, you are delaying too much – GO AHEAD NOW My son and I will bless you mightily. Child I have so much in store for you and Kathy and time is so short. Please do not delay much longer my son or things will pass you by. Philip I love you and fully understand what you are going through. Son I truly delight in you. You are a special son that has been tried and tested and I trust you. Proceed my son, proceed.*

*I asked for a sign and had an inner picture of an oyster shell opening with a beautiful pearl inside. Kathy is like this – a beautiful heart that is most precious.*

Yet still I delayed and returned to Cornwall. But then I received a prophetic reprimand *'You won't do what I've asked you to do'*.

So the season had changed from one of enquiring of the Lord to the point where He was now asking me to jump by faith or I would miss His appointed plan and timing. I didn't know that at the end of the year, if something didn't happen, Kathy was planning to return to Shropshire and walk away from the relationship. She was sensing the Lord's timing and knew we couldn't procrastinate forever and she didn't want to put her life on hold, possibly missing God's plan for her own life. However, now *the impossible had happened! The Lord had brought me to a place of absolute peace. The turmoil had gone!*

# Kathy

When I returned to Devon from Shropshire at the end of August I decided to see if this relationship was going anywhere. I was thinking that if by the end of the year nothing had changed, I would seriously consider moving up near my friend in Shropshire. I had decided I would need a total change, if things didn't finally work out with Philip.

In this thought process, it wasn't that I was doubting God or that He'd spoken but I did know that Philip really had to come to a place of being willing to get married. Not just that, but the turmoil within him had to be dealt with so that marriage wouldn't tear us apart. There had to be healing. If that didn't happen, then there really was no future for us.

So, I was back in Devon; back to the occasional meeting with Philip and the long distance relationship.

That autumn we were much more relaxed together and gradually Philip seemed to be more at peace. There was no radical moment when things eased but a slipping into being comfortable together. Philip had asked me during one enjoyable time together, 'Is this what marriage is like?' It was as if he was beginning to dismantle the lies he'd been believing.

In December, he came up to Devon for a friend's birthday party one weekend and stayed over for the Sunday. He'd been getting really good at the courtship side of our relationship and I'd been wined and dined, given little thoughtful gifts and it was just lovely.

This particular weekend, he turned up with a huge bunch of lilies and white roses. They were particularly fragrant and beautiful. I remember saying 'what's the occasion?' and he just said he wanted to spoil me. It was delightful.

So on the Sunday morning despite thick fog, we decided to take the dog up the local beacon. As we climbed up the hill, we came out of the fog and broke into glorious sunshine. It was quite breathtaking. We made our way to the beacon, which was the highest point and one built in the days of the threat of invasion from the Armada. A wooden bench is there and it's a great vantage point for the spectacular views. On this day it was quite ethereal with the low level blanket of fog where trees or the occasional house peeped up through - surreal and very beautiful.

*I was thinking it couldn't get any better than this and I asked Philip – 'a penny for your thoughts.'*

*He said he thought it was time to jump through the next hoop and before I knew what was happening, he said 'will you marry me?' I was so surprised, I quipped, 'Shouldn't you be down on your knee?' So he did – he got down on one knee, in the mud and he proposed! He asked me to marry him, holding my hands and looking me in the eyes. He looked the most whole, happy and content I'd ever seen him.*

I really hadn't guessed. I had given up so many times I was just living one day at a time and no longer running ahead. So when it finally happened, I was delightfully surprised and as overjoyed as I could be because I didn't see it coming.

He had bought me a beautiful brooch because he wanted something to give to me as a sign of our covenant but he wanted me to choose my own engagement ring. How precious. On returning home, we were greeted by the sight of a pair of white doves on the lawn outside my front door!

We both felt so incredibly happy. And so we told everyone dear to us and our engagement became official. 11th December 2005 – one year, 7 months and 2 weeks after we first met. Phew, was that a long haul!

**Lesson Learned**
**Perseverance! Love... always perseveres 1 Cor 13v6**

**We also rejoice in our sufferings, because we know that suffering produces perseverance; perseverance, character; and character hope. And hope does not disappoint us because God has poured out his love into our hearts by the Holy Spirit whom he has given us. Romans 5 v 3-5**

For my Christmas present that year, Philip presented me with a beautiful Lladro china piece of two white doves. It's exquisite. He'd bought it, 9 months previously when in Spain, knowing he'd be giving it to me for Christmas and in response to 'our' Bible verse in Song of Songs 2 v11, 'the cooing of turtle doves is heard in our land', which God had been using to speak to both of us about marriage.

And then God started working on us AGAIN!

We set a date for the wedding on 8th April 2006, 4 months away and started the planning. In my journal I wrote:

*This time leading up to our marriage is the oddest of times. Since getting engaged God has us in a hot crucible. Inner hurts, character issues, strongholds are surfacing. It's really tough. I need God's peace. Why so sad? Why so fearful? I trust You. I trust him. I partly trust me.*

Part of what was going on was the preparation for me to be uprooted. I should know! This was my business -how to manage change! By marrying Philip I was leaving my home, my church, friends and closing my business. It took major readjustment. I was also planning a wedding and anyone who's done that, knows it holds its own special stresses.

It was also the normal process of two previously independent people starting to move together to form one I'd been really enjoying my independence and not having to account to anyone. Once more I would be learning to submit and share these with another. I was less eager than I anticipated. He was also learning to involve me in decisions and his life.

The Lord reassured me one day in my prayer time:

> *You're being uprooted from all that's familiar ready to be transplanted. And after a short while of readjustment to the new soil you will thrive like you've never done before because the sun will be on you and sweet rain....It won't all be battles my child. There will be respite and such joy, much laughter if you allow it. Be of good courage. I trust you on this path, the narrow path because I know you'll make it.*

Words like this from the Lord kept me going when it was a bit uncomfortable. I was also aware the Lord was delighted over our upcoming marriage and dancing with joy over us. He certainly likes weddings!

# Philip

Andrew Baker came and gave me another encouraging word.

> *When you were a little boy you were excited about having a day out. God wants me to feel the same about Kathy, who is a God given blessing, with opportunities for fun.*

However, we began to get serious opposition as the enemy realised he hadn't stopped this marriage so far. The Lord reassured me that He was training me. Thankfully, God also sent His prophets along to encourage us both in the midst of what could have been devastation. He forewarned me of a serious assault about to happen. In my journal I recorded:

> 'The enemy will try everything possible to stop the marriage... indeed My son, the enemy will try and stop the marriage.'

*God wants Kathy and I to stay in rank. The strategy of the enemy is not just to bring us down but to divide us. In bringing us down he wants to bring division. Stand, having done all, stand. Stay together!*

In the light of these words from God, I decided that I would stand on God's promises, and sing over them and shout and laugh at the enemy, rejoicing in God's words. I chose to believe God. I'm glad God warned me in advance.

Around this time, a self appointed 'prophet', decided to intervene and bring great discouragement . This man had a dream which he believed was God saying the marriage wasn't of Him. He wrote it down and I received it by post, two weeks before the wedding. I won't give the details because they were very dishonouring of Kathy. However, the ways of testing a true revelation of God are always that it has the handprint of God's love attached, even if bringing correction. This 'revelation' had no such hallmark and was in fact accusatory and unkind.

Then three days before the wedding he left another message, this time via answer-phone. It also contradicted everything God had been speaking privately to me over the many months and which had been confirmed again and again. However, even though I knew it to be false, it did lead to real unhappiness. I decided not to tell Kathy until I'd worked through my own emotions as I knew it would really upset her that someone was speaking so ill of her, and someone who didn't even know her.

I did get some advice with regards to these words. The enemy was trying to undermine my trust in Kathy, my faith in God and my belief in myself, as well as trying to rob us of joy just before our wedding.

But each time there was an assault, I'd receive another word of encouragement.

I also took the precaution of receiving prayer to have all the horrible words the false prophet had spoken over Kathy and I, broken off, so no curse would land. We did of course release forgiveness towards him too and pray for him.

Whilst all of this was going on God was at work in my emotions, dealing with my fears of whether I had what it takes to be a husband and the deep wounds of boarding school. Praise Him, because freedom was coming.

# Kathy

The night before our wedding, Philip was saying goodnight outside my home before he left. We looked up and it was a full moon surrounded by a rainbow of iridescent colour. Suddenly I was looking into a huge eye and I remember gasping. Philip then said, can you see an eye? It felt as though we were looking into the eye of God. It was beautiful, amazing and literally awesome. It took our breath away.

We went inside but were both so curious about this phenomenon we went back outside to look again at the moon but the moment had passed and it was just a beautiful full moon once more.

# We Made it! - The Wedding, Honeymoon and Beyond

There is surely a future hope for you, and your hope
will not be cut off.
Prov 23 v 18

# The Wedding

## *Philip*

By the time the wedding day arrived, I was totally peaceful. I wasn't nervous, I wasn't anxious, I was ready. I knew that I loved Kathy and the feelings were becoming real.

Leading up to the wedding, inevitably the whole thing of the wedding night was looming a bit large. I wasn't anxious or agitated any more, but still believing by faith that the sexuality issues were dealt with. God even encouraged me directly in this way through a most surprising person. There's a lovely, very educated Christian spinster lady, now in her 80s, who runs a ministry in Cornwall. I was visiting her shortly before the wedding and we were talking about something, when she stopped mid sentence and said 'Mr Laity, God says you're worrying about sex and you're not to. All will be ok'. And then she carried on talking as if nothing embarrassing had happened at all. Well, I don't think she was embarrassed actually! Also, another dear friend rang to say she felt God would make it 'all right on the night'.

And did He? Let's just say, for the sake of blushes, both of these ladies were totally correct and we saw the miracle that God had been working during all of those months of waiting. We can now praise Him for our natural and fulfilling intimacy together!

**Lesson Learned**
**God is faithful and sometimes faith truly is spelled R I S K**

# The Honeymoon

**He who finds a wife finds what is good and receives favour from the Lord**
**Prov 18 v 22**

## Kathy

We were blessed to be able to go to Cyprus for our honeymoon, and God continued to treat us with signs of His favour and blessing. As we've mentioned the verses in Song of Songs 2 v11-12 were very special to us and we had the text as part of our wedding ceremony:

> *See! The winter is past:*
> *The rains are over and gone.*
> *Flowers appear on the earth;*
> *The season of singing has come,*
> *The cooing of (turtle) doves*
> *Is heard in our land.*

Whilst flying out, Philip asked if he could buy me some perfume at the airport. We selected one called 'L'air du temps' by Nina Ricci'. Imagine our surprise when opening the sealed box in our hotel room, to discover the bottle stopper is two intertwined doves!

Also, in Cyprus, sadly there are hardly any birds because they shoot and trap them. However, we were driving over very rough terrain and I suddenly saw two birds in a tree beside the road. Asking Philip to pull over, we were amazed to see they were a pair of turtle doves, cooing! They are distinctive with exquisite tortoise shell plumage and very lovely. We felt blessed at God's kindness in giving this amazing sign and confirmation of our wedding scripture. Neither of us had ever seen one before.

On the final day, Philip took me out in a catamaran, as he used to sail one. Before launching out into the deep, he prayed for God to send some wildlife for Kathy to see as a parting gift. He was specific. He asked for us to see either dolphins or turtles.

Within minutes of being out in the bay, a huge leatherback turtle rose up between the bows of the catamaran. I shrieked with excitement and it dived back down. But another one surfaced right behind it. They were not due in to that area for another six weeks and none had been seen in the bay that year. For us, not only was this a specific answer to a specific prayer but we knew God was having some fun with us from Song of Solomon. In the King James version of that verse, it says the 'cooing of turtles' was heard in the land and the word dove was omitted and we could sense God's smile at the play on words.

Again and again, we saw God's lavishness and love for us. Thank you Daddy! We were aware He was showering us with love and rejoicing over us with singing and celebrations.

**Lesson Learned**
**God loves marriage!**

# Others' Testimonies

**Commit to the Lord whatever you do, and your plans will succeed. Prov 16 v 3**

In the chapter following, we've included some other people's testimonies. They are all different, as you'd expect with a God of diversity. Each learned different things as they were led towards marriage. We thought their stories would add an additional element to the book and there would be additional wisdom to glean from hearing their stories too. Some 'got it right', some 'got it a bit wrong' but God helped in each case. All of them have been brought together for this 'end time' season.

## *Lynda and Bill:*

**Life after Divorce - Marriage in mid-life.**

## *Lynda*

What if?
What if Your heavenly Father gave you something beyond your wildest dreams, in a way you never could have imagined for yourself?
What if the romance of your youth became the romance of your middle age?
What if the person behind the white hair and the wrinkled skin was the same one you had loved when you were young and carefree?
What if the heartaches of the past became the heart joys and hopes of the now?
What if you unwrapped a present and found the very person you never knew you needed but now couldn't imagine living without?

If I turn the clock back 40 years, you would see a young girl madly in love with Jesus, young of faith, and head over heels in love with a handsome young fellow. He and I grew up in the same church, attended rival high schools, and went to the senior prom together in 1970. We dated on and off through high school and some of college. Then in 1973, we went our separate ways.

For almost 20 years, I was then married to a man who was both a pastor and a marriage and family counsellor. He walked away from Jesus, from faith and from our family, leaving us all with broken hearts. After so many years of marriage, the last thing I expected was to be a divorced, Christ-following woman with three teenagers to raise on my own. I could not imagine how the bills would be paid or how my heart would ever heal, much less how my faith would see me through such an avalanche of pain.

But when God writes your story, He puts the commas and punctuation in. He knows about the question marks and the coming exclamations of joy!

For twelve years after my hurricane of a divorce, I was single. Jesus became my Beloved Husband; such intimacy; such exquisite love.

During these years, I had an occasional blind date and one brief relationship from an online dating experience. Single in your 40s and 50s is very different to being single in your 20s, let me tell you! I longed to have an earthly husband, but also only wanted a man who was totally sold out to Jesus. I was content in my singleness and my contemplative lifestyle, but was also open to the possibility of marriage again after much soul care and healing prayer.

So imagine my utter surprise, when I heard from my high school sweetheart.

He found me again over the Internet. We'd parted over 34 years ago! We discovered we were living just one hour from each other, even though we were born and raised over 1500 miles away.

On our first meeting we actually walked right past each other, as we'd changed over the years apart and didn't immediately recognise each other. The date was as nonchalant as a summer breeze, nothing unique; no fizz, no fireworks, flat, simple. It was nothing special, nothing which sparked either of our interest in one another again. Seven months went by before we again saw each other, volunteering at a gleaning event for a food bank but we kept in touch by email.

When we started dating again after this, he realized that our relationship was a gift from the Lord for a new chapter to our old love story. One day, he said he thought the Lord had given us back to each other, since we'd been each other's first love. It was ours to accept or walk away from, he believed.

My fears hounded me. Would dating and loving a man distract me from the Lover of my soul? I had become a woman of deep prayer, living a contemplative life, full of silence and solitude. A retired school teacher, I became a spiritual director. Could I jump the hurdle of distrust and hurt left from being abandoned before? Would I choose to write my own ending to my story by living remotely? Would I continue to self-protect so that I would take no relationship risks?

Or would I trust God's surprise twist to my story: His offer of Bill as the man I was to walk though life with from here forward.

Much prayer, seeking wisdom from godly friends, meeting family and time with Jesus confirmed our love. We didn't rush but allowed Jesus to heal our broken hearts and restore them with hope and joy. Fear of being hurt was for me like walking a tightrope. Trusting Jesus to be the centre enabled me to walk through my fear into utter trust that this man was a good gift to my heart from a good Heavenly Father. Romance and discernment walked hand in hand. I also was watching how this man treated my heart as I stepped into the new chapter God wrote called Marriage Restored.

I learnt to trust again and now we delight in living God's invitation to love, as man and wife. I'm so glad I made the leap, so glad I allowed God in to heal the pain and so glad that I have once more the companionship of marriage. I could so easily have chosen to walk away and not face my fears.


**Insights from Linda and Bills' testimony**

**Linda and Bills' testimony is a beautiful one which clearly shows how God can bring tremendous good out of circumstances which aim to crush us. Linda found herself on her own, as a Christian – something she'd never contemplated happening. Her heart had to**

deal with a host of struggles when her first husband walked away: it broke with the pain, there was shame, there was agony both emotional and physical, children to care for, income to find plus a host of questions about how she could be in this situation.

But what I love about Linda is she ran full pelt into the arms of her Father and fell even more deeply in love with Jesus. She allowed her broken heart to be touched, restored and healed at a profoundly deep level. Then when her Beloved Bridegroom knew she was ready, He encouraged her to once more be willing to marry. This could have been the stalling point for Linda. She could have chosen to stay on her own, protecting her heart from further pain, loving her Jesus but not opening her heart to be willing to love Bill.

Instead, she chose a very hard road and a courageous one. She chose to trust a man again. She looked the issues full in the face. She confronted her fears but she also took Godly counsel and listened to those with wisdom. She didn't rush but used discernment, to check, to see, to wait and watch that this relationship did indeed have the handprint of God on it. She also observed the man carefully to see how he treated her heart.

She might have just 'assumed' it had to be God. After all they'd been childhood sweethearts hadn't they? Surely God was giving them back to each other. As it happens, He was – but she was wisely patient and careful, prayerful and discerning. She didn't just assume the circumstantial evidence meant it was God.

I love the fact she included others in her decision. She knew that her own heart couldn't be the only deciding issue in this leap of faith. As a result, when she went down the aisle to marry Bill, she was sure, she was radiant, she was excited and full of faith. She'd walked the walk of heart healing and closed the chapter on previous pain, ready to embrace the new chapter God is writing for them as a married couple.

This testimony is a wonderful one of hope after divorce, of hope for those in mid life who think marriage has passed them by and hope for those who think God has forgotten them, or overlooked them. He knew where these two individuals were and He reconnected them in His timing. What happened after that was to a great extent their own choosing. What a wonderful and happy ending.

## Steve and Nikki

Young marriage – Some things right, some things wrong. A redeeming God.

## Nikki

I became a Christian around 1983 but by the time I met my husband in 1989, I was not only backslidden but had been in an intimate physical relationship. I remember getting ready to go out one night and thinking to myself, 'Tonight I'm going to meet the man I'm going to marry'. I dismissed the thought as soon as I had it. However, before I had even laid eyes on Steve, I had asked my friend if she had a prior claim, as I'd heard about him. When she shook her head I thought to myself 'Good!'

Steve was very shy and as a 1980's girl who loved to dance I was put off a little…..not only because he wouldn't dance but also because he was younger than me. Hadn't I always said I would never go out with someone who was younger than me? I flirted with him every time I saw him and had practically given up by the time he asked me out a month later. I played it casually but was over the moon. We dated for a year and then Steve joined the Forces.

This was a real test for our relationship as he worked away during the week and only came home at weekends. Despite some tricky patches and a great deal of fear on my part, he hinted at a proposal and in August 1992 I finally accepted. We were intimate from quite early in our relationship as there seemed to be no reason not to. I regret that now, as it put our relationship on completely the wrong footing and basis.

As the date for the wedding approached, I began to really think about God again.

My parents had split up when I was 16 which had a devastating effect on me and would affect our marriage for a long time. I didn't want our relationship to end, so I began to really pray about whether Steve was the man God wanted me to marry. I prayed that if the relationship was wrong that God would end it. I was in a fragile state at this time and I told God that while I was unable to break it off, I was willing for Him to either give me the strength to finish or end it in some other way. Previous experience had shown me that when God didn't want me in a relationship, when I turned to Him, the relationship would usually come to a natural end. The strange thing was though that after Steve joined the forces, we nearly did split up many times but I could never go through with it.

The other concern was that even though I was returning to God and seeking Him again, Steve was very 'anti-church' having been 'made to go' when at boarding school. I had been brought up to attend church but Steve's family were (and remain) 'weddings, christenings and funerals' people. His only concession during this time was to attend midnight mass on Christmas Eve so that we could exchange presents first thing on Christmas morning. He was happy to get married in church but that was it! However as I continued to pray about our relationship and desperately seek God about my future, I found myself promise God that 'if' Steve and I got married, I would go to church every week....without fail....no matter what he said or what the consequences were. It's important to include here that I was in no way trying to 'blackmail' God. I really wasn't sure that He wanted us to be together. The prayer was just part of many desperate and heartfelt prayers I prayed around that time.

You can imagine my shock then, when Steve turned around one day on a Sunday drive (after we had attended church to hear our marriage banns read), and said, 'I think when we get married we should go to church every week!' I never told him that I had been praying about our relationship or that I had made that promise. I answered him casually, 'Yeh if you like' but inside my heart was dancing as I took this as a sign of permission to marry him. We married in April 1993 and are still together, 19 years later. Steve told me some time later that he was aware of a 'God-thing' happening in me at that time.

We kept the promise we made that day and have attended church faithfully ever since. Steve didn't become 'a Christian' until 1996 but he faithfully sought God in the intervening years. This is not to say that our marriage has been an easy one or that we have never struggled. I'd like to tell you that we have had the most amazing God-filled marriage. On the contrary we came very close to breaking up on more than one occasion but our continued relationship with God has healed and mended and cemented us in so many ways. We have four beautiful children and today Steve is well known as a strong Christian, a man of integrity, honesty and righteousness - a leader in the body of Christ.

## Insights from Steve and Nikkis' Testimony

We included this somewhat unorthodox testimony because it is so full of the heart of God in working His ways with people. Steve and Nikki admit that they didn't go into marriage following the Bible guidelines. Initially they were 'unequally yoked' with Nikki a believer and Steve a seeker. They also had intimate relations before the wedding. However, within their story we see a heart submitted to God's way. Nikki gave up the right to the relationship. To the best of her ability, within the framework of her own childhood hurts and insecurities, she was honestly willing to allow God to end the relationship and she would have accepted His decision. This took a huge amount of courage, bearing in mind she'd already let her heart go to Steve. She knew she was meant to marry a believer, but God gave her a clear sign of the future with Steve.

Within their testimony you can also hear how Nikki would have preferred they had followed God's way from the beginning and no doubt they have had to work through some issues as a result of this and the other 'baggage' which they both brought into the marriage.

The redemptive nature of God though, has brought this couple right through to a place where today they are both in church leadership positions, they shine with Jesus, their love for each other is very evident to those around them and their children are thriving within the loving family atmosphere.

# Nicoleta and Callum

## Surrendered lives, God directed from across the globe

# Nicoleta

God has brought Callum and I together from different parts of the world in the most unexpected, yet the most natural, ordinary way. Although he is from New Zealand and I am from Romania, we did not need to use the Internet or other means of fast communication across distances – we met in a friend's house in Plymouth, UK. However, to get here God had to take us both through a journey. I had to get a job in the UK six years earlier, and even before this, to train as a social worker in order to get this job. Also he had to prepare Callum, bring him to England and direct him towards where I was. Although this seems quite difficult at a human level, it's nothing for God – He holds this earth in the palm of his hand and all the earth is His.

When I first met Callum I did not think anything of it – he wasn't necessarily someone who would make me fall in love at the first sight. This was a good thing, because gradually God revealed to me who Callum really was and all the beauty inside him, which is the one that lasts forever. I remember a friend of mine saying - 'the beauty passes, the ugliness not'. The meaning of this being – the outside beauty passes but the inside ugliness remains, so look for the inside beauty. My mum also used to say to me – 'you will soon get used to the look of a man, handsome or not, but you will never get used to an ugly character'.

So, going back to Callum and me – God revealed to me who he was: his creativity, his caring attitude, his sensitivity, sacrificial nature, his humour and much more. All these characteristics were what I was actually drawn to, even without realising it.

However, I was not intentionally seeking a husband, although sometimes when I met someone I would wonder: 'God is this the one You have in mind for me?' I remember my mum saying - 'What is going on? Why are you not finding a husband? You are 30 years old...' (although she has never put pressure on me, which I always appreciated). I would say to her – 'I don't feel like praying for a husband, I am happy as I am, I just want to pray that God will do His will with me and use me for His Glory, and if He needs a husband for this, then it will happen – I trust God'. I strongly believe that you have to get to this place before God gives you a spouse, otherwise you will be a burden for them as you seek to be 'completed' by them; only God can complete someone.

So, Callum and I spent time together with other friends until it became clear that he liked me. Then, we decided to meet and talk about it. I prayed the night before the meeting and asked God 'What is this? Is Callum the one You want for me?' The answer came straight away (which surprised me): 'He is the one I want for you, don't miss the opportunity'. I heard this clearly and I couldn't even ask again, in case I misheard or fabricated myself the answer; I knew, I had peace and went to sleep. We met, talked, agreed and never looked back. All Callum said was in perfect harmony with what I wanted and believed – harmony and peace is God's hallmark. 16 months later we got married and I can't thank God enough for his wonderful gift. I know He shows His love for me through Callum's love and as long as we base our lives and relationship on Him, we are safe. It's a great adventure!

However, it wasn't easy to get to this point. I realise now God used good and bad things in my life to change me, so I grew in my knowledge and love of Him. He showed me my real nature and how much I needed Him by allowing me to be bound to someone else I loved for many years but who was not free to be with me. I now know, He was holding me in his arms and protecting me. These years I lived in the valley of the shadow of death - He never let me down; he was so patient and loving and forgiving.

Moreover, one year before I met Callum I thought I was in love with a friend, only to discover that he was in love with someone else. I remember crying for half a night when I discovered that. Little did I know at the time what wonderful plans God had for me. I imagine Him looking at me, thinking 'how silly you are...if only you trusted me...I know everything...I know what is the real deal for you and it's all in hand - trust me! You are so precious to me that I want the very best for you!' Anyway, the tears helped – the tears always help in my case and I cry a lot. For me the tears are a sign that God is near – a deep emotion which makes my tears roll down unstoppably.

This is my story – Trust and love God with ALL your heart and all the other things will be given as gifts from the One who knows you the best and knows your future – He is the best Father and He always gives good gifts to his children.

# Callum

When I met Nicoleta I had recently moved to the city after two very hard years which had pushed me to the limit and beyond what I thought was possible. A relationship with a woman was not in my top 5 things to focus on. I was happy being single and was prepared that should God want me to be single for the rest of my life, then I was happy with that. However, whenever I met a new person I would secretly wonder if this was to be 'the one'. But I wasn't actively looking to 'settle down'. I'd previously read books on relationships such as 'Men are from Mars, Women are from Venus', 'I kissed dating goodbye' and 'The 5 love languages' but these were more about understanding the differences between men and women. My parents had encouraged me to pray for my wife since I was a teenager, but I'd seldom done this as it had been a low priority. When I did pray however, I would pray that God would prepare us for each other. Thinking about this now, I realise He answered that prayer most successfully. One bit of advice from 'I kissed dating goodbye' was to avoid having a relationship just for the fun, to try, or because I was bored. My next relationship would be started with the intention of it ending in marriage. That meant whoever I was going to begin courting, had to be a woman of high value.

Arranging for two people from opposite sides of the Earth, to meet in a different country, and be there at the exact right time is something only God could pull together. Nicoleta and I have both acknowledged that we were not ready to meet each other even six months before we did. God still had preparations to do. For me, it was about ensuring I could trust God even when everything else said it's the wrong thing to do. God ensured He came first in my life.

After a while, I began to notice special qualities in Nicoleta not found in other women. I had a 'list' which I'd previously been advised to ignore, and as a relationship wasn't one of my main priorities, I'd not paid much attention to it. But gradually as I got to know Nicoleta, the 'boxes' began to be ticked. We had many similar interests, but more importantly; she was passionate for serving God, something I'd come to value highly in the previous year.

When I decided to make a commitment to Nicoleta and see if she would be interested in courting, I pulled on some of my experiences and books that I'd read to create a set of standards I wanted in a relationship. Not rules in the burden sense, but a set of foundation principles which I thought were important to ensure the relationship was going to stay on the right track and head in the right direction. This included making it a relationship of 3: Nicoleta, myself, and God. He would be the glue which held us together. He had to remain central. I also risked rejection by telling Nicoleta I wasn't interested in dating for fun, but in pursuing a relationship towards marriage. Yes, the big scary 'M' word. But I wanted her to know I was serious about this. When we met to discuss our relationship, I 'laid my cards on the table' and told Nicoleta how I felt and what I wanted to do in a more serious relationship if she agreed to join me. I was quite prepared for her to say 'no', but I was going to give it a try. Nicoleta's 'yes' meant we began a step in the direction toward marriage, and as we continued to meet together each week and pray, we could see how God was confirming everything for us.

It just so happened that my parents were visiting when Nicoleta and I had been courting 5 months. Mum gave me her approval quite unexpectedly. It was good to know I had my parents' support. We'd also had a few people who thought we were already married because of the way we looked 'comfortable' around each other. The relationship had always been fun, no difficulties, and it was a contradiction to the idea that relationships were hard work. Nicoleta became my best friend.

Before I met Nicoleta, I thought I was fairly together. Not in the sense that I think too highly of myself, but that I didn't think I had many problems. However, being with her brought out a few insecurities I hadn't encountered being single. God had to work through this and it wasn't easy. But it was worth it. I wanted the best relationship, not an average one, so I was prepared to do what I could to improve, thus becoming more like Jesus. I have found a direct connection between a struggling relationship, and a lack of time spent with God. Whenever He remains central in my life, my relationship with Nicoleta is good. There is a lot of responsibility on my behalf to focus on God. If I don't, my marriage will suffer.

Moving from courtship to marriage has been a smooth transition. After a full 9 months of preparation for two weddings in two countries, we've been able to get back to what we enjoy the most – serving God with our gifts. We've had to draw the line in some activities to ensure our relationship comes first, and while this has meant adjustment for others, it has also been a time of blessing as God has opened up more wonderful opportunities to be used by him – not separately, but as a couple united. As long as we keep our eyes focussed on God, being where He wants us to be, being obedient to Him even if it's not what we'd prefer to do, and putting Him first, the stress of the future fades away, and we hold on for the ride. It makes it exciting and completely rewarding.

### Insights from Nicoleta and Callums' Testimony

**It's so beautiful when you see a couple come together totally led by the sovereignty of God. With both Callum and Nicoleta their minds were focussed on Jesus and becoming more like Him and serving Him. Whilst both of them wondered about marriage it was not a preoccupation, nor a particular focus. They were more intent on pursuing God first. I can't help think about the verse 'Seek first the Kingdom of God and all things will be added unto you'. (Luke 12 v 31) As Nicoleta mentioned, she knew she had to get to a place of being willing to be single or married and content in either. She makes such a wise point that only God can complete a person, no man. To get this understanding means they come together as whole people, with what they can give into the marriage rather take out.**

Callum's honesty about the boundaries of dating and his intention to treat women properly is refreshing, in a culture of picking people up and putting them aside. He wanted to honour the woman he believed God was calling him to court and potentially marry. He's not saying that he was definitely right, but by the time he started to court Nicoleta he was more or less certain in his mind that this was a courtship to marriage, not just fun dating. They already knew each other and the friendship blossomed into more.

All the way through, there is a sense of peace, God's order and two surrendered souls, sold out for God. Wonderful.

# Mike and Gill's Story

## Friendship and Second Opportunities

# Gill

Mike and I met at our local parish church, Holy Trinity – a good place to meet someone who shares your faith! We had both recently finished long term relationships and so were not in any hurry to get tied up. My relationship had been with a non Christian, as it had started before I was "born again".

Mike and I became good friends, despite there being an age difference of 13 years. In actual fact, age was never an issue for us and I don't think we even asked each how old we were for quite a while.

We soon found that we had loads in common, were from similar family backgrounds and values, as well as sharing the same sense of humour. One of Mike's less subtle comments to me on seeing my photo was, 'You look like Olive Oil' (from the Popeye cartoon!) I still married him.

From the outset of our friendship we were always honest and open with each other. There were no pretences or hidden secrets, including the fact I was told I couldn't have children. Our friendship grew, as we did things together, such as going to Christian conferences, music events and on holiday. But, we didn't live together!

It was always important for us that we were accepting of each others' differences and differing interests but having said this, we learnt to enjoy some of each others' past times. I took up shooting, Mike being very keen and he was willing to travel to France, a place I enjoy visiting, as I'm a fluent French speaker and teacher.

During our courtship, we also shared and supported each other through some difficult times, including the illness and death of both of Mike's parents. Thankfully, both sets of parents accepted us and Mike says I was the first girlfriend his mum had really liked.

However, despite our ages (Mike was 41 when we married), we certainly didn't rush into things. With hindsight, we probably could have married earlier! After over 4 years courtship, we did contemplate splitting up and going our separate ways. I felt this was the only move I could make and told Mike so. However, he felt immediately that this was wrong and told me so. He couldn't imagine us not being together. Neither could I. At that point, we knew that if it was wrong to split up we needed to make the relationship permanent, as we couldn't drift on without direction. Mike asked me to marry him in November 1985, though we agreed not to say anything, as we wanted confirmation and knew the Lord could do that without us advertising the fact.

During January 1986 we regularly took an elderly lady to visit her husband who was quite ill in hospital after a stroke. They were both lovely mature Christians and we would always pray together before we returned home. After one such visit, Cyril prayed an amazing prayer that almost seemed to assume we were going to get married. Both Mike and I separately wondered if the other had told Cyril and Kay of our plans – we hadn't, so when we shared the reality of the situation with them, it became so obvious this was God's confirmation to us. They were delighted and agreed to keep things secret until our engagement announcement on 14th February.

I can't exactly remember the timing but certainly before we went 'public', Andrew Matthew, our vicar, who was never one to be slow in speaking up, came to see Mike and asked him about our relationship. I think he was very keen to see us married. He and his wife were delighted when we did and I lived with their family for the 3 weeks prior to the wedding, as I'd sold my house and obviously wouldn't move in with Mike until we were married. Mary enjoyed almost having a 'daughter' getting married from their home, as they had 3 boys themselves.

The number of people, especially our Christian friends, who on hearing of our engagement expressed their delight, was further confirmation for us.

Because we'd both had previous relationship issues, we received some counselling from Christian counsellors, as individuals and together, prior to the wedding. We didn't want to carry these issues over into our marriage.

The weekend of our engagement, we attended a conference led by Colin Urquhart in Plymouth. During prayer ministry there, we both received assurances from God that all was in His hands. This was particularly in relation to the fact that I couldn't have children, which I'd been told when I was 19 and Mike already knew.

Before Mike met me (many years before with a previous serious girlfriend) he had been very keen to get married and have children. Yet amazingly when we met and he heard my medical prognosis, he says it was as if the Lord had anaesthetised him. In fact we went on to have two boys, who were born after prayer and a prophetic word. They bring us great joy, even more so because we didn't know they would be part of our married life, when it began.

It was a little odd, as many of Mike's friends were already grandparents when he became a parent (but then several of my friends were too, having married very young). Does it really matter if it's in the Lord's plan any way? I wouldn't have it any other way!

### Insights from Mike and Gills' Testimony

**Mike and Gill came into their relationship having both had previous serious relationships. They recognised the need to build a good friendship before moving forward, but also that their previous involvements and the fallout could affect their own marriage. As a result, they sought out wise counsel, to ensure that they were**

starting their married life without previous issues arising. When realising they were almost at a stalemate, Gill was the catalyst in bringing forth a resolution. Either they split or move forward but they couldn't continue drifting. This was quite a leap of faith but it also brought the confirmation which they wanted and the reassurance from God and through His people.

It's a lovely testimony because Gill's issue of childlessness could have been a stumbling block for Mike. He wanted to be a Dad, but he was given grace to marry Gill, knowing it was unlikely because of her prognosis. In effect, he laid that desire down on the altar. God resurrected it miraculously with the birth of their two boys. Neither of them knew this would be the outcome and they had to be content to be a couple without children.

But they knew enough about each other, their shared interests and values, as well as their faith, to know the friendship was a secure one, in which God was central. This was a strong and solid foundation for their marriage.

## John and Becky's Testimony

Beautiful endings and beginnings

## John

I grew up in a Christian home and with those values instilled into me. At 14 I became a Christian but for four years, was what I'd call a 'silent' Christian. I didn't grow and so was going backwards. When I turned 18, a Faith Mission evangelist came to our church, preaching on Jonah and 'the word of the Lord came to Jonah the second time'. I knew this was God calling me to follow Him wholeheartedly. I gave my life totally over to Him from then onwards.

I wanted to be married, I definitely knew this but I also knew that it wasn't right to date non-Christians. Even in the period between 14-18 years old, when I wasn't growing as a Christian, this was my attitude, so although I fancied girls at school I never followed through on it by asking them out. Prior to meeting Caroline, my wife, I only had one girlfriend, which lasted one month when I was 17.

By 18 I had really been discipled for 6 months and was stuck into service for God. During this time I went to a meeting, where I saw Caroline for the first time. I was smitten. She was singing a solo and I immediately liked everything about her. From then on I just couldn't get her off my mind.

Our paths kept crossing naturally over a five month period, as our churches joined together for regular events. At this point we didn't know each other but I put myself in a position where this could happen naturally.

However, the Free Methodist church was holding a series of meetings over 4 days, in Lancaster in Ashton Hall. During this time, I targeted and pursued her, keenly chatting her up. I remember she turned 17 during these meetings. She went home after the 2nd night and told her Dad that she would be asked out the next night. She was right. I offered to drive her home. She didn't immediately accept, saying she had a lift, so I had to make it clear, I wanted to drive her home. She accepted. We lived 35 miles apart. So, I took her home and it was the beginning of the relationship.

Everything was going fantastically for me. I was settled in my mind about her, without being aware of what she was thinking. From her perspective, she was only 17 and not wanting to settle down at that young age. She was wondering 'What do I do?' She chatted with her best friend who suggested finishing with me but Caroline couldn't think of a single reason why to break off, so she didn't.

After about 4 months, I was intending seeing her at 7.30pm one evening. I set off but broke down on the motorway and in those days of no mobiles I had to walk to the nearest telephone kiosk. Eventually I managed to get a neighbour to tow me off the motorway but I didn't get home until 10.30pm.

For Caroline, she just thought she must have got the date of our meeting wrong until 10pm when her parents came back from a meeting. My parents were there and had told them I'd set off before them. She was now extremely upset and it was in that half hour she realised she loved me, when she thought something awful must have happened. Thankfully, I rang her at 10.30pm when I arrived home. That one half hour was the major turning point in our relationship.

After 9 months I was travelling home one day, convinced I'd marry her. It was then that I felt God say 'Will you give her up?' It was such a shock that I travelled home in tears. During the three quarters of an hour journey I didn't give a response. Nor the next day at work which was terrible. I knew I was wrestling with God. Eventually, that next evening I knelt beside my bed and I said 'Yes Lord, I'm willing to give her up'. I opened my Bible at random seeking comfort and my eyes fell on, Proverbs 5v18 'rejoice in the wife of your youth'. It proved to be very much an 'Isaac' moment for me, with God giving her back to me after my total surrender.

The next time I went to see her, I asked her to marry me. She immediately said 'Yes'. We were married 2 yrs 4 months, from when we started going out.

Caroline and I were married for nearly 25 years. She died from cancer, which she had for many years prior to her death. I had entered the ministry and was pastoring a church. When she was dying I went through a dreadful wilderness experience and I told the church, being open before them. One Sunday I knelt before God and my congregation just crying out for His help.

(The rest of John's story follows a little later on, after Becky's story)

**Lesson Learned:**
**John was taken by God to the place where he had to actually be willing to give up his relationship with Caroline without knowing that it was merely a test by God. That total surrender is something God often requires and not many are willing to be this obedient, yet great blessings flowed out of this for John and Caroline.**

# Becky

I was brought up in a Christian home and also believed I should, as well as wanted to, marry a Christian, so I didn't date casually. However, I wasn't a well rounded individual, being shy and self conscious as a teenager. It was only at college that I had my first brief date but the whole idea of a dating relationship scared me. Even though I'd always wanted to get married and have loads of children, I wasn't ready for it. He started to get serious very quickly and I ran a mile. I felt really upset over this for a long time. It wasn't a good first experience. Over the next three years we flirted with each other and it was a bit on-off but we didn't actually go out again.

I was friendly with a college friend who had a similar interest in classical music. It didn't lead anywhere, because the moment I got wind of his intention to ask me out, I hid! Then I fancied someone else, who wasn't interested in me and actually married one of my friends. During this period there was a non Christian who I became friendly with through amateur dramatics. When he eventually asked me out, I had to explain that I couldn't because I was a Christian. He was really good about it and we remained friends for a while. I was grateful to God for the way He worked this out and I could see He was honouring my desire to marry a Christian.

One summer during college years, I went on mission to Northern Ireland and there was this American on the team with amazing piercing blue eyes. I really fancied him. He encouraged me, even though I later realised, he had no intention of following through with me. He promised to write but he never did. He'd played with my feelings and this devastated me. I spent years getting over this. It totally rocked me but the downside was my reaction. It seemed to kick me off into flirting and I enjoyed getting men's attention.

**Lesson Learned**
**It really is a question to ask, when considering dating or flirting with someone else – are you playing with them in a way which isn't honouring? Are you being righteous in your behaviour to them, or just satisfying your own fleshly desires? The fallout for Becky was devastating because she believed him and as a Christian, she should have been able to trust him, without worrying about his motives. How sad that she couldn't and how sad that it caused her to move into the very behaviour pattern which had hurt her.**

I had been determined to marry young. However, as I wasn't, disappointment began to rule my twenties. Around this time, I decided to work abroad and ended up going to Sri Lanka with CMS, joking with my friend that I was bound to meet and marry a doctor there.

Whilst in Sri Lanka, an African man, who I knew from church approached me. He said he'd looked around and chosen me for his wife. He said, God has said 'She's the one'. I said 'No! He hasn't told me'. That was the end of that but it was a bit shock.

**Lesson Learned**
**Becky responded very maturely to this advance. People often find it hard to counteract the statement 'God has said' because it doesn't leave any room for a different opinion. For a less mature Christian, this could have caused really serious confusion and heartache. A better approach would be to say something like, 'I think the Lord might be leading us together. What do you think?' In this way the other person is considered and honoured too, but also has the opportunity to say 'no'.**

However, whilst working for CMS, I was overseen by a male member of staff, who was widowed. There was a significant age difference, over 20 years, but he took a fancy to me. Sadly, I encouraged him. I was training in counselling and he asked me to practice my counselling skills on him, thus he drew me in. He was relentless and I encouraged him - until he asked me to marry me. Then I ran because I knew I was soon coming home, and managed to extricate myself from him. I'm not proud of my behaviour but realise it was a symptom of where I was at in my vulnerability.

**Lesson Learned:**
**Even at the time Becky knew it was never a real relationship. Spiritually they were in different places. He was very liberal and high church, she was evangelical and low church, also she never intended staying overseas. She was drawn to him because she was lonely, homesick, vulnerable and isolated, as well as being flattered by his attention. Sadly, she broke his heart. It is never a wise**

situation to have a man overseeing a single (or indeed a married) woman on a regular basis or vice versa. It allows too many opportunities for wrong emotional attachment.

When I was 30 I moved to live in Salisbury and God led me to both a job and flat. On the first floor was a divorced business man, who wasn't a Christian and a lot older. It just didn't cross my mind initially, that there would be anything more than 'hello'. However, he invited me to supper one night and we hit it off immediately. For the next eight years, we were very close friends. I realise that very early on, I made an unwise decision, but we had a great time. It was borderline platonic and I knew I was walking a bit close to the edge. He wasn't a Christian but showed a great deal of interest and ironically, would always argue for the Christian message in discussions.

Underneath all this, I was bothered though and would wake up in the night and think 'What am I doing?' I was spending so much time with this person that many other people thought we were a couple. This did annoy me especially as I was now dating through Christian agencies and he was supportive of this. But there was a massive soul tie connecting us to each other. In a way, I was playing mind games with myself and in denial about the reality of the situation. I was active in the church. I felt accountable because people knew about our friendship. I felt I wasn't hiding anything and was being open about it. But it concerned me they mistook us for a couple. I actually wanted someone to say something, or challenge me. No-one did. People trusted me.

**Lesson Learned:**
**It's interesting that Becky was uncomfortable with the depth of this friendship and actually wanting someone to challenge her. Because she needed the relationship emotionally, it was much harder for her to walk away unaided. How different things might have been, had she pulled back earlier because someone had asked the right question kindly?**

What changed? In October 2003, I knew I had to make it clear, that we weren't really a couple. I was worried (I was 38), the years were passing very quickly. In the evenings I would walk home from his flat and if I thought ahead into my future I felt trapped. I couldn't imagine how things could change.

One evening I decided to stop it. We went to a dinner dance together and another guy showed an interest in me. He was not a Christian but I used that opportunity to show I wasn't part of a couple, by giving this other man my phone number. Obviously it didn't lead anywhere but it was the beginning of the end of the platonic, unhealthy relationship.

It still took me four long years to get emotionally detached – it had become like a co-dependent/pseudo marriage even though we weren't living together. I had some counselling to help me because I knew I was stuck. When he started to see another woman I sought some more help because it was causing me desperate pain. The pain was very physical and I was now approaching 40! Basically I was walking through a grief experience, with the loss of this friendship. Having the counsellor acknowledge my agony was the most helpful thing she could have done.

I went through a process of clearing things out which he'd given to me and I wrote a lot about my feelings. This included writing a letter to him, (which I never sent), as part of the grief process but it didn't really make me feel any better at the time. However, God saw my intention to let go. I also wrote down what was and wasn't true, with relation to facts and feelings and lined this up with what God says in the Bible. This was the start of seeing things more clearly.

At the same time, I was trying to meet Christian men and used an agency but each time it turned out to be a one off date and a huge disappointment. Also, deep down, I didn't really want to meet my husband this way. For me, it just wasn't romantic. This period of my life was very hard, as I undid the mess I'd made and allowed God to lead me back on course. If I'm honest, it didn't feel like He was giving me much help but in hindsight I realise He must have been carrying me and protecting me, nevertheless those years were extremely painful.

**Lesson Learned:**
**Sometimes our own desires lead us into unhealthy relationships and poor decisions. Sadly, we are then left to walk through the consequences, which can be painful BUT God can and does still give us many more opportunities to make right choices.**

# *John*

Caroline had always said I would remarry. In speaking in this way, she was giving me her full permission. She'd say I wouldn't cope on my own and she knew me very well. Also, I love being married. I am one of the greatest advocates of marriage.

The church I was pastoring was fantastic. They didn't trying to fix me after she died but they did care. They gave very practical help, gardening for 12 months, cooking regularly, cleaning, ironing and I even had a mother figure who I could ring day or night.

Deep down, despite the depth of grief, I think I knew I would remarry. Only 10 days after the funeral, my son asked me whether I would and I replied 'Mum said I would'. He seemed to have no problem with this.

Caroline died in March 2007 and in September I talked to my daughters about the principle of remarrying. But I told them I wouldn't marry without their permission for the particular person. Also the mother figure had right of veto.

When it came to actually marrying I also got my Pastors Cabinet, which is a body of church leaders within my denomination, involved. Part of their responsibility is my wellbeing.

But, I wasn't looking for anyone at that stage. It was far too early after Caroline's death. I had a date in my mind, thinking I'd leave it a year before initiating anything.

I wanted our children to know this and that I would be having a private 'Goodbye Ceremony' on what would have been our silver wedding anniversary, in the church where we married. She died 23 March the ceremony was on 23 October 2007.

In my private ceremony, I took photos with me, of our whole life together, right from the early days to the very end when she had no hair. There were photos of all our children at different ages in a chronological history. I went through it step by step. I went through the vows we'd made and thanked her for fulfilling her vows as I'd fulfilled mine to her. This was real closure. I even spent five minutes applauding her and thanking God for her. This was all building up to taking my wedding ring off and putting it back on a Bible (as I'd received it from a Bible). I found myself using a form of words I'd not premeditated, which was a complete end of the marriage, placing the ring on the Bible, and knowing it was very symbolically significant. As I went away, I felt emptier, something was missing that had been present. That bit of her that had stayed with me, now left.

I went through a very painful experience, which was not of my doing, when I filled out the tax return and got to the status I had to fill in – I desperately wanted to write married but HAD to write widower. That broke something inside of me. It was indescribably painful but a hurdle I had to go through. It helped with the anniversary releasing and admitting I was no longer married. It also, although I didn't necessarily see it at the time, made way for the next season in my life but before that could happen things got worse.

In the November my father-in-law died. He was like a dad to me because mine had died when I was 21. I went into freefall grief for Caroline again. He died very quickly, with just a short illness. By the end of that year I was truly hacked off with God.

On the last day of the year 2007, the church had a welcoming in New Year service. All my church and biological family were around but I was extremely lonely. Yet, something very special happened that night. There was a little five year old girl who also had cancer. She and Caroline were going through treatment at the same time and were bald together. That night she came over on her own and extended her hand to me to dance. It was so poignant. In that room full of people, she alone sensed my loneliness. It was a real gift to me.

So, coming into 2008, I was not in a great place.

I meet every six months with two male friends, just to share our lives together. On 4 January 2008, I was due to meet them. I found myself kneeling at about 8am by my bedside in my prayer time and surrendering everything to God. It was a very deep and meaningful time: total surrender. In the afternoon, we took it in turns to share with each other, where we were at. I shared that I would like to remarry, but was not in any hurry to start looking, wanting to get the first anniversary of March 23 over first. I said though, that I had no clue how to find someone. Being a pastor it's really difficult because you are so involved with your own church. One of them said he knew several single women and started listing people's names - he suddenly stopped abruptly, silent, then said 'But Becky's the one.' That got my attention. 'Why?' I asked. 'Because I think she'd make a very good pastor's wife.' He showed me a photo of her on his laptop. On the strength of what he'd said which was highly significant and her photo, I said I'd like to meet. As friends, we were planning our next meeting just a week before 23rd March and I thought this was near enough to the anniversary to be ok. I suggested he mention it to her a little in advance, so she'd be free for coffee, while I was in the area and we could meet to see if there was any chemistry between us. Then my friend broke all the guidelines I'd carefully put in place with regard to the 23rd March by talking to Becky within a couple of days of us being together in January.

# Becky

In the last year before I met John, in desperation I asked God to speak to me while driving to work. 'Tell me something today, anything, even something I'm looking at'. In front of me was a Waitrose lorry. Now, I've felt that God has seen me as a 'rose bud'. He seemed to be clearly saying to me 'Wait, Rose.' I couldn't take my eyes off the 'Wait'. It felt like a moment when God breathes a word of life. I can do that, I thought. If He's telling me to wait then I'm waiting for something! It ignited my faith and every day after that, I continued to praise the Lord and wait, on my way to work.

After these rocky few years, I found myself entering the new year of 2008, in a new position, with my heart raw but healed of much of the hurt from the previous relationship. I'd been away over New Year. I was upset wondering if this year would bring any change but prayed 'I give this year to You'. I knew I was back on track, a bit tender but spiritually there. I remember on 4th January, about 9.30am saying 'All to Jesus I surrender'. It's amazing this was just an hour and a half after John had made exactly the same heart prayer.

On 6th January 2008 I was in church and really wanted to sit on my own, but a friend and one of the leadership team asked me to sit with him and his wife, saying he needed to talk to me afterwards. I assumed it was about church business but he said it was something private.

So, later he said he'd met this man who was lovely and he thought we might like to meet up. He told me all about John and how wonderful he was. I was under the impression that there was some immediacy to get in touch. He gave us each other's contact details – emails, telephone etc.

It didn't really resonate with me at the time but I felt a stirring that it could be significant. I left it, expecting John to email. However, I later found out that John was livid because the contact details were released too early and he'd been keen for this not to happen. For five days John didn't do anything. Eventually I emailed him and then went away over night. I was back the next night and there was a reply. John didn't want to correspond by email and he'd sent some possible dates to phone.

We arranged 9am that Friday morning. We talked and had a conversation which was highly significant. I decided there was nothing to be gained by pretending so was brutally honest. I was 43, life hadn't worked out as I'd wanted and I'd messed up but I still trusted God for the bigger picture. We spoke for an hour and the conversation went very deep. We even discussed getting married and having a baby.

We began to speak regularly. John thought it would be weekly but found after that first phone call on the Friday, he could only wait until the Sunday before talking again. Then phone calls became very frequent and we began talking about everything.

About three weeks into this, I suddenly started to panic. I realised how much I loved Salisbury, my church, my friends, my work. Reality was kicking in, that I would have to leave all of these behind, if this relationship worked out.

On 16th February, we finally met, a month after first speaking. We met in a church where I was on holiday and away from John's area, so that we wouldn't bump into anyone who knew us.

# John

I suddenly realised we had been speaking a lot on the phone. I was now moving in a relationship to a point where I needed to know that this was God's leading. I hadn't even met her but already knew this could be serious.

So, I'm kneeling beside my bed with my Bible open in front of me. I was really praying, 'I need to know. Is this your will for me? I need to know because if it's not, I need to stop this.' My mind immediately went to Prov 5 v 18 the verse God had used to confirm that I was to marry Caroline. I was thinking wouldn't it be wonderful to open my Bible again and have a verse clearly speak like that time. But my rational mind kicked in and argued against this. I was after all, a mature Christian of many years now and God couldn't be expected to move in the same way again. I opened my eyes and looked down. My Bible was open at Prov 5 v18. I was amazed. It was like God was smilingly saying 'Is that clear enough?'

Nevertheless, this was scary as we hadn't yet met.

**Lesson Learned:**
**Note how John was acting on faith, recognising God could be leading him and Becky together. Before going any further, he checked with God and was willing to only move if he knew it was the right way. There was no guess work involved. He sought God before he let the relationship move into something more serious.**

# Becky

I was now praying that God would perpetuate our relationship or stop it. If it was Him I would walk in it. However, at this stage, I would have laid it down, yet I also knew already, that this felt different.

**Lesson Learned:**
**Note how Becky was also prayerful about the relationship and willing to let it go at this stage, before her heart became more entangled.**

So we met in the church and I was a bit nervous thinking what are we going to talk about now, we've done so much talking on the phone. What'll it be like face to face? Do we hold hands? However, he walked in and smiled directly at me. I was not dressed up at all, in my old Barbour coat, really not looking my best as my holiday accommodation was basic. I now know John hated that Barbour. Despite this we spent nine hours together. In a very cute little ceremony in the church, John asked me out officially as his girlfriend and he sang me a song he'd written.

# John

I thought the relationship was much further along than it actually was, when we met. However, mentally Becky was ready to move on but emotionally not quite as prepared. Her heart was held back. I truly wondered, could Becky have the capacity to love me? This was a very difficult weekend for me, as we were not as far forward as I had thought from our conversations and yet I knew God had already spoken to me.

# Becky

On the Sunday, I had arranged to go John's church incognito and have lunch with his mother figure. So when I turned up with my friend, I said we were just visiting. However, she recognised me. Instantly, I had love for her. There was a heart connection.

During that service, I was reminded that in my heart of hearts, I'd wanted to marry a full time leader and a worshipper. I fell in love with John during the service, as I saw him worshipping God and heard him preach.

Afterwards we went to lunch with the mother figure and her husband. John and his daughter joined us. On a walk in the afternoon, his daughter was so kind when she said to me 'You are not the enemy'. I felt so accepted by them all.

My greatest challenge and the most potentially threatening thought process was comparing myself with Caroline. I absolutely had to refuse to do this. I could not compare. We were very different people and I wasn't going to compete. John never made me feel this way, it was a pressure I put on myself. I couldn't quite believe he was so over her. I would think, 'How can he love me so much after such a short time of her death and 25 years marriage.' However, I wasn't threatened by Caroline and he really had worked through his grief.

# John

I made a decision not to initiate talk about Caroline but wait for Becky to ask questions but she wanted to know about Caroline, so would ask.

I felt it would be wise to go through the marriage preparation that Becky's church put on, which any couple heading towards marriage would go through. It seemed advisable. It was during this course that the strong emotional attachment to Becky's friend of 8 years was unearthed.

# Becky

It was a difficult moment when we started to talk about this former friendship and I had to be totally honest, did I still love this other man? John asked me and I knew I had to deal with it there and then and with any residue from this relationship which had been so consuming. I was devastated that I couldn't give John the immediate answer he wanted and needed but I took time to ponder it. This took a while, even though I knew I loved John. When I was sure I then told him. I know he found that period very difficult, whilst waiting for my response.

# John

During the marriage preparation the issue of this former friend had to be addressed and I asked Becky 'Do you still love him?' This put me into turmoil. I couldn't have proceeded into marriage, if she was unable to leave that relationship behind and fully commit to me. I'm convinced that if this hadn't been unearthed during our marriage preparation, it would have put considerable pressure on our marriage and caused problems. However, within a few days, Becky had worked the issue through and was able to say she loved me.

I don't think most of us are called to be single but it's learning to be content in the waiting. We are waiting for God to move. Waiting is worship. In the natural realm we also have to be emotionally available, as well as physically available – not too busy for a relationship and we are wise to deal with our 'stuff' with either ministry or counselling. Someone who is disgruntled with God or anyone else, is really not attractive. Happily, having completed the marriage preparation and faced the issues which came up, we were able to move forward.

# Becky

On April 9th, John proposed to me in the church where we'd met. From the moment I was engaged I loved it and was amazed how different it felt from being single. I found it so much easier to relate to people with the pressure being taken off, I could be myself and I was therefore happier.

We married on 18th October 08, just 10 months after we'd both spoken on the phone, and in the same year where we'd surrendered our whole selves to God.

**Insights:**

**At every step John and Becky maturely addressed the issues in their relationship prayerfully. They submitted to God, to other people,**

to each other and were humble enough to accept input from others, even though they themselves were both mature leaders. This led to a very strong foundation being developed, over a short period of time and a great foundation on which to build a solid, God centred marriage. I love the fact that an intermediary was also used to bring them together, one who knew them both well and could see them potentially together.

# PART TWO

Listen to advice and accept instruction, and
in the end you will be wise
Proverbs 19 v 20

May God Himself, the God of peace, sanctify you through and
through. May your whole *spirit, soul and body* be kept blameless at
the coming of our Lord Jesus Christ.
1 Thessalonians 5 v 23

So I say live by the Spirit, and you will not gratify the desires of
the sinful nature. For the sinful nature desires what is contrary to
the Spirit, and the Spirit what is contrary to the sinful nature.
They are in conflict with each other...
Galations 5 v16

# Pitfalls in the Preparation Season

In this section we will be exploring some things which prevent people marrying. It may expose some pain, so before we go on let's pray.

*Lord, please help me as I read this chapter. Gently highlight to me what you are saying. I offer You my fears, blindspots, defence mechanisms and every hindrance which would cause me to react and not be open to Your prompting. I let go now and trust You. Please speak where I need to hear. In Jesus' name. Amen.*

We realise our marriage journey is just one story. Many readers will have been patiently seeking God for a partner. You do not feel called to be single, are faithfully serving God and yet, the desire of your heart has not been met. Along the way, you have doubtless learnt many lessons on how to walk with God in the area of relationships. We acknowledge this and we know that the pitfalls we refer to will not apply to every reader.

Therefore, as we offer some insights, it is not meant as comprehensive coverage. We are aiming merely to expose possible hindrances.

The following observations come from our own experiences as single people, our circle of single friends, and Kathy's work as a life coach with a Christian singles website. We find there are three main areas to be mentioned:

**1. The physical**

**2. The soul (mind/will/emotions)**

**3. The spirit**

As we go through these, if you find yourself getting defensive, we suggest you take it to God. We are not finger pointing. The aim is to expose lies, behaviours and attitudes which are not helpful in fulfilling dreams and destinies. We're on your side, cheering you on and longing for your heart's desires to be fulfilled but sometimes (and this won't apply to all of you), hard truths cut before healing comes. We both had to walk through this and can say honestly, it's worth it!

# The Physical

Whether we like it or not girls, a man normally does his first tracking of a woman by what he sees and if he likes what he sees then other things progress. He was made by God to be visually attracted. However, men, this needs to be submitted to God's guidelines and not the world's. With media pushing the visual and pressurising women to conform to a certain size and looks, it can easily creep into a Christian man's perspective.

We hope it goes without saying that looking at pornography pollutes the mind and the eye gate of your soul. God is quite clear: 'Do not let sin reign in your mortal body so that you obey its evil desires.' Rom 6 v 12. 'Let us behave decently; not in sexual immorality' Rom 14 v 13. If you have a problem in this area it may be a stronghold which you need to seek help for and accountability to break free. In this connection, we recommend the 'Freedom in Christ' programme, in the Appendix, which is excellent in stronghold busting.

Pitfalls in the physical realm are very real and can be a bit discouraging. On the websites for singles, including the Christian ones, many men in their 40s and 50s state they are looking for a person 10-15 years younger than themselves. Perhaps this is because they are still hoping for children or perhaps they are putting too much emphasis on the physical. Just ask yourself; why should a 30 year old lady consider a 45 year old man? Unless God is directly leading, this is the unusual scenario not the usual.

Can you see how the enemy has twisted a very natural part of a man's makeup, his appreciation of a woman's appearance? Of course, the media, internet and the tabloid press, has much to answer for in this connection.

However, if you are a man and you are balking at what is being said here, we humbly suggest you ask God if He is pleased with your attitude to women. Does it line up with scripture, in respect to honour and kindness? If it doesn't, repent and ask Him to change you, then be willing to change.

Many people have a list of what they want from a marriage partner. Now this in itself is not necessarily wrong. It can be a faith focus, if it is compiled prayerfully with the assistance of the Holy Spirit. However, if it's a list of your wants, consider submitting it to God, knowing He knows best of all and what you truly need. He is much wiser in His choices than we are.

For instance, you may say you want someone blond and tall, slim with blue eyes. What happens if God's ideal partner for you is shorter, squatter and of a different culture. Is this a problem? Is there an area for surrender here? Is there an area of trusting God? Many people lose out on God's best spouse for them because they insist on a particular size, shape and appearance, and will not move from this.

I'm being deliberately provocative because many people box themselves in and do not even 'see' a person God has placed right in front of them, because of a prescribed way of thinking. At the end of the book are some questions to deliberately challenge some ways of thinking which may be hemming you in.

Now, when I met Philip, I wasn't immediately attracted. I had always liked dark haired guys and he's blond. He has a tall lean physique and I was used to broader. But you know what, at some point my attitude and how I looked at him changed totally. I could have dismissed him on these initial points and really missed out. Now, I'm totally in love with his physique.

Likewise, he could easily have looked at me – shorter than average, rounder than average, middle aged and thought similar things. Men, especially if you're not a spring chicken yourself, you should perhaps consider being more flexible about appearance, so that you don't miss out on God's choice of partner for you. In the long term, it should be remembered that the physical is only one small part of a marriage.

However, having said that, it's no excuse not to present yourself at your best. Basic hygiene is obvious but you'd be amazed how often this is overlooked, especially if someone's feeling a bit low. Good breath, deodorant, clean hair, hands, clothes, nails are all important. Sometimes, these can be blind spots and we encourage you to ask a trusted friend some pertinent questions, after you've read this chapter – ask them about your personal hygiene. It's a brave friend who would bring the subject up if there is a problem, but it's easily remedied once you know.

Sometimes, there are also coping mechanisms behind which we hide subconsciously pushing others away. This usually happens if we've been emotionally or physically hurt – and let's be honest, most of us have at some point. There is help and I would recommend the list of helpful people and organisations in the Appendix.

On a practical level, meeting people today isn't that easy, especially once out of full time education. It depends on your local church, where you live and how extroverted you are. But one thing's for sure, staying in will not help you. You have to be involved in something and when you want to meet a Christian, it's more likely they'll be involved in Kingdom business too. So get on out there.

I can almost hear the barrage of remarks to that last sentence and the comebacks people are saying. Maybe some are really excuses. Now I say this as a neutral statement with no accusation or condemnation because I've been there. I've hidden away, with all sorts of reasons why I couldn't do this, go there, or participate in something because… I even convinced myself they were true. But they weren't. They were usually based on fear. Fear of being rejected, looking a fool, not fitting in, not having anything to say, being too old, too fat, too whatever……can you hear the lies, the defence mechanisms? I wonder what yours are? We all have them. Sadly, when we are lacking confidence around others of the opposite sex, our words don't give us away, our actions and body language do.

Body language is key. Everyone picks up on the bristly person, defensive, aggressive through posture not even words. It's unattractive and not many people will persevere to get through that brick wall. Likewise, head hanging, hiding behind glasses or long hair, not making eye contact is all giving the signal that I don't really want to engage with you – whereas inside you might be longing to. Can you see what I'm saying? We project our fears through our bodies and through our posture. It's almost like having a label on our forehead or hanging round our bodies saying 'out of bounds' or 'come any nearer and I'll bite you!'.

I'm spelling it out in black and white because these points will apply to some people.

If you want people to be interested in you, be interested in them and be interesting - with no other agenda than that. It's not hard to learn, practice. If you've really no idea where to start, seek out a Christian coach who works in this area and take some sessions with them. They will work to your agenda and can help with things like confidence building and interaction. I well remember coaching a young lady who lacked confidence in conversation with men. We would practise on the phone and she became a great conversationalist. It was only a few weeks before she was out and about socialising happily, having learnt a new skill and that's what most of this is, learning a skill. It's not out of reach and old habits can change - if you want them to.

If you are involved in something which interests you, you naturally meet people with similar enthusiasm. It also gives you a point of conversational interest other than yourself. Philip and I met at the Healing Rooms training. We both had much common ground to talk about with regard to the healing ministry. From that our conversation could branch out.

Passivity, self-pity or apathy will not bring you any nearer to your marriage. Nor indeed will super-spirituality. Sitting in night after night doesn't do it. I haven't yet heard of someone having a word of knowledge to knock on a stranger's door and ask them out. (I can just see someone reading this, who has this exact testimony! Well, if so, I'd love to hear it). However, most of us are just not that bold and we will more than likely wait, disappointed, forever. We might also have put the restriction that we are not going to 'do' anything but wait for them to 'come' to us, to our church etc. Of course, if our future mate has also prayed that prayer and is acting on it, then it gets no-one anywhere. It can look really spiritual not to be 'looking' when it may be fear rather than faith. Blaming others for your situation is also extremely unattractive.

By 'getting out there' I'm not using it in the crude term of putting yourself about. I mean get involved in something where you will meet Christians and that you're passionate about. Enthusiasm is infectious. In the Appendix there are some resources, such as social networks and websites. If there's nothing in your locality, someone has to take the initiative and start something. Maybe that could be you. The more single people you know, the more you'll get to know, as you introduce each other to your friends.

These are just suggestions. If you are really stuck, then look again at the Appendix for ministries which will be able to help you and minister into the wounds or struggles which are locking you in. There's no shame in seeking help.

Just an aside and this applies to both sexes – work, sport, business, family, even ministry can become all consuming and the total focus of life. To have a relationship, you will have to make room in your life to accommodate one. Be careful, especially men who compartmentalise and become focussed on doing, not to exclude social and fun events where you relax and unwind. Make room for love and laugher. Lighten up!

If you decide to go onto a Christian social website, do read their guidelines for your profile. If you get stuck on what to say about yourself and don't feel you are interesting, ask a good friend for help. Ask them to list things about you that you can then weave into something interesting and informative. Also, use an up-to-date picture, which doesn't mislead, and is realistic. Men, if you're beer swilling, involved in extreme sports and dressed in fancy dress in your photo, it's a great way of saying I'm not ready for a relationship, I'm still happy being single and having fun. Be sure your photo is representative of where you want to be going, not just where you've been.

I know much of what we've written above sounds obvious to many of you. Please forgive us if we seem to be stating common sense. But we also know there are those of you who do find it helpful to have things spelled out.

# The Soul (mind/will/emotions)

**Trust in the Lord with all your heart and lean not on your own understanding.**
**Prov 3 v 5**

We know that the battleground is in our minds but the trouble with that is we're often blind to our self-sabotage.

If the enemy can get us to believe a lie, he's won. He doesn't have to work any harder than that because we will follow through on our thought processes. Each person is targeted uniquely but I have seen a trend among those wanting to be married which include lies such as the following:

- There aren't enough Christian men to go round, so there's bound to be more single women left.

- I'm too old (can be said by someone in their 20s or 80s. My mum remarried at 70 and was happy for 10 years with her husband before she died).

- God said it's not good to be alone, so what about me? He's left me alone. Be careful not to imply God's a liar? This will undermine trust, so be honest and put it right with Him.

- I might as well marry a non Christian, otherwise I'll never marry. What's wrong with that, as long as they're supportive of me as a Christian?

- My body clock's ticking, I must find someone quickly (I've heard young women in their early 20s saying this) and if I love him, it doesn't matter he's not a Christian. I might lose out on having children.
- I've never even had a date, so there's not much chance for me!

These are just a few examples and don't forget, you only need one person to be with – *the right one!*

Likewise, I've also talked with men who approach the whole marriage issue as if they are buying a car. They have a list concerning the possible woman and logically discuss her attributes and failings. She'll be excellent at this but not this. They then go on to argue themselves out of even exploring the relationship let alone progressing through to commitment because she doesn't match his list exactly. Unlike most other scenarios in their lives where they make decisions based maybe on an 80% sureness of the rightness of the decision, they are looking for 100% absolute certainty. But with the things of God there is always an element where He's looking for faith and trust in Him.

With women, I've encountered on many occasions the fantasy scenario. I see it where someone runs ahead, dreaming of the wedding and the future. This shows itself by dwelling on plans for a wedding, dreaming of where to get married, looking at dresses, places for receptions, even beginning to gather things for a home. Sadly, I've even seen a lady make a wedding dress believing she was going to marry a man on a certain day. He hadn't even asked her out. All of it was in her imagination, but couched in super spirituality ('Well God has said', which blocks anyone being allowed to comment).

Another was determined she was going to marry 'Mark' in 'May'. She was living alone and began to get rid of her furniture and empty her freezer. She hadn't met 'Mark'. She never did meet 'Mark' and she became so defensive when cautioned that she cut off all communication. She'd believed a lie and saw it as faith. These are extreme examples but sadly not that uncommon. If these people had only been willing to check their 'guidance' with others and been open to input, a lot of heartache and disappointment would have been avoided. It's not lacking in faith to talk it through with others.

A man does not want you fantasising about a wedding, on your first date, or worse, before you've even spent time together. He will run a mile. Be warned, he can almost smell a desperate woman and will be put off.

You might also want to be aware of a very practical point. If you always go around with the same person e.g. your close friend, and you attend church and social events together, you may find it very hard to meet someone. It takes a confident man who will approach two girlfriends who are close emotionally. How does he find a way in, to talk with them. So, if you go to an event together, what about sitting separately, so you have to engage with new people and have conversations with different people? It's about making room for a new person in your life.

Men it's the same for you. No girl is going to approach you in a group of men (unless she's particularly self confident). Make it easy for her, and girls, make it easy for him to approach you. He might be just as lacking in confidence in this whole relationship area as you are. Give him all the openings he needs to strike up a friendship.

Conversationally, keep it light and not intense, especially when you're just getting to know each other. No long self history about your woes and troubles, or sob stories. Men, you can unwittingly manipulate a soft-hearted woman by sharing your tragic story and it's not fair. It's playing on her emotions, to give you sympathy. It can really hurt them in the long term, if you've no intention of pursuing the relationship. Even so, bad history and sad things can wait until you know each other a bit better. Generally speaking, it's often better to have light hearted banter and fun when just meeting.

Now, what about misinterpreting signals? This is another minefield but one where Christians should stand out from the world in our exemplary behaviour. It is not appropriate to flirt and play with another person's emotions so that you feel great. It is not kind to give someone special attention with no intent of following through. Men can be a bit naïve on this. Let me give you a bit of inside information guys. If you start to spend time with a girl, going on walks, maybe inviting her to join you for a film because you're at a lose end, seeking her out to talk through confidences – she will assume you are interested. You may just be treating her like a mate, but she will certainly not be reading it like that. Please, one on one time, male to female is a minefield waiting to erupt with hurt feelings, unless you make it really clear where you are coming from at the outset and keep reinforcing this.

For instance, I had a good friend who was a widower but he knew I was in the beginning of a relationship with Philip. There was a clear boundary. I am not available. But we enjoyed friendship and time together, knowing there was nothing more. However, men, again be warned: many women will not be able to hear the 'I only want to be friends' line and will still think you are interested. It's just the way women are made, to let our emotions get engaged, just as you do your visual sight.

So be careful about running ahead of God. If you've done this in the past or have a tendency to daydream, submit it to God. This also applies if you think you've been misled by someone. Let it go. Let go of your judgements of them (we're not allowed to hold them) and forgive both them and yourself and maybe even God, if you feel He was involved (a faulty thought, but we can get a bit muddled).

**I charge you... do not arouse or awaken love until it so desires.
Song of Songs 2 v 7**

Let's talk a bit more about the emotional. We've touched on some issues above but another area where it can be dangerous for Christians is when you are in ministry together. For instance, in many prayer and healing ministries there is usually a couple involved, i.e. a man and a woman, not necessarily married. This can lead to an intimacy and closeness due to the nature of the help being given to the person coming for ministry and the need to work as a team. It can lead to strong emotional ties, which in their turn can lead to false assumptions of closeness. We've both experienced this scenario and been led down false trails of broken hearts and heartache for us and others. Be careful and keep yourselves professional and accountable. Whenever you are working closely with someone of the opposite sex this is a danger. If it's happening in your work place and you are being drawn towards a non Christian of the opposite sex, get yourself out of the situation before your heart gets entangled and 'yes' that might mean a new job. At the very least, keep yourself accountable to someone – just share and ask them to pray. Often the pressure lifts because it's been brought into the light.

The emotional side of relationships can be a roller coaster of despair and hope. It is hard and I'm not pretending there isn't hurt along the way, especially if you've been waiting years for a mate to come along. In no way am I belittling the pain of that waiting period. I know only too well that 'hope deferred makes the heart sick' Prov 13 v 12. I was childless after 14 years of waiting, at the point when my first husband died. I do know the pain of waiting with unfulfilled longing. But I also know there are some lessons to learn, which I wish I'd learnt before I lost some friendships along the way.

I'll use my scenario about childlessness because it does resonate for some women in their 30s and onwards. I'd been trying for children for years and kept miscarrying. The pain of that childlessness was intense and gut wrenching. I was surrounded by friends and family producing babies and if I'm honest, I couldn't cope. I was on overload in my emotions. I couldn't seem to get through the pain threshold and it would overtake me in totally inappropriate ways and at dreadfully inconvenient times. My reaction was to withdraw, lick my wounds and basically hide. I lost the ability to rejoice with friends who were pregnant and it stopped me interacting with their children and enjoying the times with their families. Now, I'm being vulnerable here. I'm not proud of my behaviour and I'm not proud of the depth of pain I went to. My focus was totally on having my own family and I couldn't get past this.

Then Geoff was killed when I was still in my 30s. Four of my closest friends and family were pregnant. Not just that but 9 months later I had to have a hysterectomy. Having children was over for me, but the pain wasn't.

It went on and on and on. It made it impossible for some of those friends with young kids to come near me. I had my defences in place, behind which I nursed my pain. I didn't know this was what I was doing and I didn't know how to get out. I felt so isolated because most women make friends locally with parents of other children. My friends were either 10 years older or younger.

Over the intervening years, God has drawn near and healed this part of my life. As I've grown deeper in love with Him, I've allowed Him on many occasions to deal with the hurt, the sense of betrayal and loss of not feeling a real woman. I'd allowed it to make me feel less than a woman, somehow.

Can you see the lies I believed? I'm not a real woman. I'm not cared about by God or other people. I've the worst life ever. Yuk, self-pity is one of the most unattractive things out there. Lose it. It will put everyone off, including your closest friends and family, as will moaning. Take it to God, off load on Him and then get the focus off self and out on to others. Of course, occasionally you will still need to 'dump' the pain with a close friend but don't let it become a habit.

You know, it can always look as though the grass is greener on the other side; that everyone else has a happier, more blessed life; that married people are in a league of their own happiness. Lie. There are as many unhappily married people as there are unhappily single people. The married state is not the issue here. It's the state of our own heart in relation to the life God has given us and where He's chosen to place us. Thankfulness will unleash the blessing and lavishness of God. He loves us to be grateful for what He's given us and not always be going on about what we don't have.

And on that note, did you know we do not have the right to be married? We do not have the right to demand anything of God. We are to be humble in our attitude, thankful, presenting our requests to Him and leaving them there. I remember the 'Youth With A Mission' teaching on marriage which is so sound. As a single person you know that God loves marriage and that His normal route is marriage not singleness. However, He also asks us to surrender all our agendas, plans, dreams and rights, to Him. That includes marriage. If you can let go of the right to be married and leave it in God's hands, He will then either release you into marriage in His season or give you the grace for a call to singleness. (I personally believe the latter to be very rare and those people I know who have been called have a peace about the calling).

If you have not done this, I urge you to do it now. In praying the following prayer, you release marriage and let it go, with all the pain of loss that may accompany this, saying you'll trust God with your life, knowing He is good.

Pray with me now:

*Dear Lord, I bring before you the whole issue of marriage. You know how much I've longed to be married and have my own family. It is a deep desire of my heart and there is much heartache attached to this desire. However, Lord, I choose today to relinquish every right and demand that I have made to be married. I want to say that I will leave it up to you whether I marry or not but that I want to do your will above all. Lord, I surrender my life totally into your loving care, including this desire. Please, in your time would you release me into marriage if it's your will for me but if it's not, please would you give me the grace to be peaceful and fulfilled as a single person, knowing this is your route for me. Help me to trust and have faith. In Jesus' name I ask. Amen.*

Well done. That's not an easy prayer and you may need to revisit it from time to time. It's a real Isaac prayer (like when Abraham was asked to sacrifice his only son to God) only you don't know if God will intervene or accept your sacrifice of singleness. Whichever He does for you, know that out of His immense love and goodness, He will lead you into what is His perfect plan for you.

I wish I had done this with the children issue. It would have saved me years of heartache. I'm not saying that from time to time I still don't long for children of my own. I do, especially now many of my friends have grown up children heading towards being grandparents. It's an area of life experience I've missed out on totally and would have thoroughly enjoyed. But am I bitter about it? No. Am I wistful about it? Sometimes, a little. I know I can be fulfilled in many different areas which I couldn't have if I'd had children. Did God deliberately make me childless. No, I don't think He did. Things happen. The Fall happened. We live in a broken world where bad things happen. But, in it all, He will walk through it with us and that's the key. We can use the experiences to grow and be more Christ-like or we can stay in the pain and turn inwards becoming bitter, resentful of married people, desperate, self pitying and most unattractive. Don't put your life on hold waiting for marriage. Grab it with both hands, live it to the full and if God brings a partner along, celebrate and rejoice.

So, in all things set yourself up for success. Catch those runaway emotions and thought processes which are keeping you in a box. Face and identify the fears which are really excuses for inaction. Get additional ministry help if you're really stuck and have realistic expectations. Not every Christian woman can marry a Christian leader. Some have to marry the ones willing to direct cars, do acts of service, and acts of kindness behind the scenes. Not everyone will marry a mature Christian. Some will have to be willing to come alongside a new disciple in marriage and grow together from there. Can you see some of the sides of your box yet? Don't set yourself up to fail.

# The Spirit

**So I say, live by the Spirit and you will not gratify the desires of the sinful nature. Galations 5 v 16**

**...those who are led by the Spirit of God are sons of God. Romans 8 v14**

A few times during our courtship, I sensed the Holy Spirit witnessing with my spirit that God was drawing us together. This was especially apparent when involved in spiritual activity. For example, when we worshipped side by side for the first time in Philip's church, we both felt God drawing us together. On another occasion, when driving along the motorway praying in tongues, we suddenly found we were both given the same prayer language. This has never happened before or since. Clearly God was up to something.

For a Spirit filled Christian, don't be surprised if you find yourself recognising your future spouse supernaturally. Often God's way and the world's are opposite. With the world, relationships tend to start with physical attraction and then the soul realm.

We have mentioned throughout the book that there is a spiritual battle surrounding Christian marriage.

For our struggle is not against flesh and blood, but against rulers, against the authorities, against the powers of this dark world and against spiritual forces of evil in the heavenly realms.... Ephesians 6 v 12

The thief comes only to steal and kill and destroy. I have come that they might have life, and have it to the full. John 10 v 10

As these words of the Apostle Paul and Jesus indicate, sometimes the devil may have footholds in our lives that are blocking us from becoming married. For example, if you can see a pattern in your family or extended family of people being single who wanted to marry, it may be a curse coming down the generations. Also, there may be unconfessed sin, such as previous ungodly relationships that have not been repented of.

If any of these issues apply, we recommend you get prayer ministry in your local church or at one of the specialist healing ministries mentioned in the Appendix.

Another pitfall in the spiritual realm is acting too rashly when we receive a prophecy concerning marriage. We would caution that prophecy is most often confirmatory in this situation and not directive.

The following two scriptures may help with regard to this:

**For we know in part and we prophesy in part. 1 Corinthians 13 v 9**

**Test everything, hold on to the good. 1 Thessalonians 5 v 21**

If you want to be married, always get your guidance first and foremost from God directly, most often through scripture and allow the prophetic to confirm to you what God is already saying.

Why do I say this? Mainly as a safety precaution. I have met too many lovely Christians who are holding on to a 'prophecy' about marriage which just hasn't come to pass. They haven't asked God for confirmation, seeing this as lack of faith. It isn't. It's really good to get confirmation through other prayerful people and through scripture. And should you need to get further confirmation about something, including a marriage prophecy, I would suggest you ask people other than those closest to you. Your best friend, however loving, has all sorts of emotional involvement in your situation, as do your family. It will be very hard for them to hear from God objectively because in the soul realm, there will be other things in operation for them i.e. consequences in their lives if you do marry and adjustments to be made. Nobody chooses change. So they might not be able to be as objective as you need.

When I've needed confirmation about a subject God is speaking to me on, I've enlisted prayerful people whose discernment I trust and whose walk with God is mature. I've usually not told them the situation I need them to pray about but just say, 'please I need additional confirmation about a situation I'm facing. Would you be willing to ask the Lord if He has anything to say through you, regarding Situation A?' I'm not putting pressure on them, just asking them to listen to the Lord. I find it such a helpful thing to do. Over and over again, the confirmation will come through or alternatively a warning not to proceed.

Be alert about situational guidance, visions, dreams, prophecies which can so easily be open to misinterpretation. Circumstantial situations will be read through the filter of our own desires.

Scriptures can also be used by the enemy to mislead. He knows the Bible. He tempted Jesus using scripture. If you're a passionate seeker after God, he may try this one on you. Philip believed the scripture that he was 'one called to be single' Matthew 19 v 12 because it fitted into the self defence mechanism he had successfully built around himself. God had to dismantle that whole fortress before he could move ahead.

Of course God will confirm through scripture but He will also confirm through an inner witness of peace. Cultivate closely that relationship with the Holy Spirit, so we are sensitive when we move against His will. Peace is an indicator of whether we are in God's will. This is the deep peace which is there irrespective of circumstances. A lot of the turmoil Philip experienced was in his emotions but he hadn't learnt to separate it from the Spirit's peace. Learn to listen to your inner peace in situations other than relationships, so that you are familiar with the Holy Spirit's prompting in this area. It will then be easier to recognise His leadings regarding a relationship.

God is always faithful to talk to us about issues which relate to our heart. He's interested. He's compassionate. He's loving but He won't be manipulated by our moaning and demands. He responds to our honesty but above all to our faith. He loves faith. So once He speaks, hang onto that truth and use it against the enemy who will come and say 'Did God really say that to you?' He'll confirm it, if you lose your assurance. Keep being teachable. Keep humble and keep allowing people to speak into your situation with correction. Even if you think they're wrong with the advice they're giving or they come over clumsily, have the sense to ask God whether there's any truth in what they are saying. There might just be and we don't want you to lose out because the messenger messed up.

So, having said all of the above, we also know there will many faithful and surrendered Christians who are still in the 'waiting room'. We commend you. Keep praying, keep trusting, keep enjoying life to the full and loving God. Your destiny ultimately is in His hands.

# Provocative Questions

**The heart of the righteous weighs its answers. Proverbs 15 v 28**

The following questions are designed to show if you are open to the leading of the Holy Spirit in the whole area of marriage or whether you still have boxes around your thinking. The aim is that it will reveal whether you have truly surrendered the whole area over to God. Don't forget, He is kind and loving. If you are still finding there's resistance, go back to the prayer of submission earlier in this chapter and pray it again. You might want to add in the proviso, Lord make me willing to marry someone who.......and relate it to the question below which pressed a button e.g: make me willing to marry someone of a different race; who is older than me; who is shorter than me; who doesn't have a ministry. You get the drift. So, here are the questions.

Would I be willing to marry someone, if God was leading me who:

• Has a different educational background?

• Is a different race?

• Has children and a large extended family?

• Doesn't want or can't have children?

• Is divorced with an 'ex' or widowed?

• Is called to overseas missions or travels a lot with their work?

• Lives in a different part of the country or world?

• Has a different or no clothes sense?

• Wouldn't easily fit into my extended family?

- Has no wage and lives by faith?

- Have different interests from me?

- Is sick or disabled?

- Is from a different denomination?

How would I feel about the following scenarios?

- Am I willing to relocate nationally or even internationally and leave behind my family, friends, local church, home, job and social life?
- If I have adult children would I be prepared to leave them behind or ask them to move out?

- Would I be prepared to give up my job and independence to have a joint life?

Now in asking these questions, it certainly doesn't mean God is going to require this of you. It's merely an exercise to open up your thinking. Some of these questions will provoke answers and reactions of 'I couldn't possibly do that' and the reason may be totally legitimate. God knows you and your circumstances. He will only ask of you what is necessary but he will challenge you where you are holding on to something which He wants you to let go of, so you can move forward into the next phase of your life – marriage.

**In his heart a man plans his course but the Lord determines His steps. Prov 16 v 9**

# Questions To Answer Honestly on Meeting a Potential Someone:

**Make plans by seeking advice: Prov 20 v 18**

**Do not be unequally yoked together with unbelievers…. 2 Corinthians 6 v 14**

- Do they love the Lord Jesus Christ and put Him first in everything?

- What is God saying to you?

- Does this person display the fruit of the Spirit? Galations 5 v 22

- How much of your lives overlap, in terms of interests, spiritual walk?

- What areas of major difference are there? Are these important?

- How do my friends and important people in my life relate to this person?

- How do they relate to their friends/family?

- Where are they on their healing journey?

- What is their calling in ministry? Does it overlap? Is it a problem if it doesn't?

- Are you/they willing to relocate if necessary?

- What are your similarities?

- What is their attitude to money? Do you have the same values?

- Are they willing to go through a marriage preparation course?

- What are your areas of conflict?

- What is their attitude towards the relationship? Are they prayerful?

- What am I drawn to? Is it more than the physical?

- Can I see myself living with this person in old age?

- Am I willing to seek wise counsel and let others 'speak' into the situation or do I get defensive?


These are just jumping off point questions. Many of the issues would be worked through in a marriage preparation course, which many churches now run. Alternatively, we recommend you go through the 'Marriage Book' by Nicky and Silu Lee.

# Biblical Examples of Marriage

So what does God have to say in the Bible about marriages of destiny? Are there incidences where He ordains people to marry or does He always leave it up to the individual to make that choice?

## Isaac and Rebekah: Genesis 24

Abraham wanted a wife for his son, Isaac. He sent his servant back to the place where his family came from. There is a clear supernatural element to this matchmaking. Abraham said *'God will send His angel before you* so that you can get a wife for my son from there'. (Gen 24 v 7 *emphasis added*). On reaching the land, the servant prayed specifically (Gen 24 v 12ff) and God clearly led him to Rebekah even without her knowledge. However, the servant prayed knowing that God was sending him to find a particular woman, handpicked for Isaac. His specific prayer was; 'she will say to me, "You drink, and I will draw for your camels also"; let her be the woman whom the **LORD has appointed** for my master's son.' (Gen 24 v 44 NASB *emphasis added*) Rebekah did all the things he'd prayed, so confirming she was God's destined wife for Isaac.

It is amazing that she was willing to leave her family and trust in God to marry a man she hadn't even met. It seems difficult for us in our culture but this is a clear example of a marriage of destiny ordained by God. The marriage appears to be blessed and happy; 'he loved her; and Isaac was comforted after his mother's death'. Gen 25 v 66

## Ruth and Boaz: The Book of Ruth

Ruth was a young widow who had suffered extreme sadness and famine. She decided to honour her mother- in-law, Naomi and said 'where you go I will go and where you stay I will stay. Your people will be my people and your God my God.' Ruth 1 v 16. They return destitute to Bethlehem where Ruth has to work, trying to feed them both. She goes into the fields, to pick up the left over grain behind the harvesters. At this point she discovers she is in the fields of Boaz, a relative of Naomi's dead husband. There has been a divine leading and already Boaz has heard of her faithfulness and goodness to Naomi. He says to her '....may you be richly rewarded by the Lord the God of Israel under whose wings you have come to take refuge.' Ruth 2 v 12.

There is a clear indication of the overshadowing hand of God in the circumstances which bring Ruth and Boaz together, including the assistance and wisdom of Naomi.

Not only did Ruth leave behind the death of her first husband, the famine of the land and the heartache of childlessness but she became honoured and blessed above many, even being listed in the genealogy of Jesus.

## The Wrong Choices:

Sadly, we also see the consequences all too often of when people don't involve God and choose to make their own decisions without consulting Him. David ravished Bathsheba and murdered her husband. The son of their union died as a result of David's sin. Samson was led astray by Delilah, only to lose his strength and the fullness of his destiny and die young. Abraham tried to 'help' God along in fulfilling the prophecy of children, by sleeping with a servant Hagar and birthing Ishmael. How those consequences continue even to our current day!

We believe that God calls people together for specific purposes which we can't fulfil as individuals.

# Our Marriage so far

## *Kathy*

So how is our journey going so far? Philip and I are already into our 7th year of marriage as the book goes to press and it's been a marvellous journey. I am so thankful that God has brought us together. Does that mean it's been plain sailing? Actually no. We've had our ups and downs, like any marriage. There have been adjustments, not least two mature people who were previously living independent lives learning to think as 'we' and no longer 'I'.

Personally, I had to relocate and leave behind my friends, church, locality and close down my business. Even though I've moved around the country a number of times previously, this time was somewhat harder and it took me a while to settle into a place where Philip had grown up and knew so many people, whilst initially I knew no-one. However, with perseverance and the knowledge that God asked this of me, it's been easier as time has gone on.

Philip adapted to marriage remarkably easily for someone who'd been a bachelor all his life; and despite those who said he'd find it hard to adjust, he hasn't really. He often comments that he wishes we'd married years ago and he hadn't realised he was lonely because he kept himself busy.

We are both aware that God uses us to disciple each other and that "iron sharpens iron" Proverbs 27 v 17. Like any process where God decides to prune his children, this can hurt. For us, it often happens in areas where we respond in completely opposite ways. We have both been quite independent and used to taking responsibility. I'm spontaneous, creative and prefer to be unstructured. Philip is logical, thinks through the details and enjoys routine. It's inevitable that we sometimes bump up against each other. It's taken a while to realise that although we do things very differently, for instance in how we make decisions, neither is necessarily right or wrong; just different. We are growing in patience and appreciation for our differences, as well as learning when it's wise to compromise.

However, we love being married. We can highly recommend it. It is rewarding and fulfilling. We love being together facing the future with God, hearing Him reveal His purposes for us as a couple, whilst still retaining our individuality. We laugh a lot and have great fun together.

## Philip

When I first shared with my curate that I felt the Lord was leading me to marry, he replied: 'Philip, marriage is the quickest road to sanctification!'

I have pondered this statement, and in our time together I can see God working to shape our characters, knock off rough edges as we learn to interact together.

The Bible teaches us the importance of dying to self and considering each other more highly than ourselves. We are encouraged to *'Give and it will be given to you. A good measure, pressed down, shaken together and running over, will be poured into your lap. For with the measure you use, it will be measured to you.'* Luke 6 v 38. When we have been tempted to be selfish, or we start to harden our hearts to each other, we both find we lose our peace and experience a distancing from God. As soon as we repent and ask each other's forgiveness, a joy and lightness is quickly restored.

One area we have been particularly tested in is our health. We have both suffered with chronic fatigue (M.E.), periods of insomnia and for Kathy some life threatening illnesses that have resulted in a number of hospital admissions. On these occasions, it made me realise even more how much I love her, and it has also brought us closer together when I have had to support her practically through healing prayer.

You will have gathered that Kathy and I are very different. I tend to be more 'left brain' focusing on detail and reasoning. She is more 'right brain', intuitive, creative and able to see the bigger picture. I believe our differences bring greater balance and enrichment to our lives, for which

I am so grateful. God has given us grace to appreciate our differences, as well as to honour and encourage each others diverse gifts.

A lesson that we are learning is that the more we give and lay our lives down for each other, the more we receive back in return. The world tends to have a more selfish approach, such as 'what is in this relationship for me?' Clearly, this is contrary to the teachings of the Bible, where in Ephesians 5 v 25 it says, 'Husbands, love your wives, just as Christ loved the church and gave himself up for her…'

On taking an overview of our courtship and marriage, I can honestly say it has been the most fulfilling (and occasionally challenging) period of my life so far. I would not have missed it for anything and encourage others to take the plunge, if God is leading you into marriage. I can truly vouch for the truth of the following verse in Proverbs 18 v 22, 'He who finds a wife finds what is good and receives favour from the Lord'.

## In Conclusion

Our prayer for you is that this book will have encouraged you to keep praying, keep believing, keep seeking and keep trusting God to bring you together with a marriage partner. We are praying that He will initiate many marriages which have a divine destiny and that His enjoyment as a matchmaker will continue to be fulfilled.

In this time when we believe God is moving in power across the face of the earth, we passionately believe He is calling His people into God ordained marriages ready for the very end, the time when Jesus will come back for His beloved bride and then there will be the marriage celebration to top all celebrations. Until then, we know God loves marriage and is *for* you! Contend for your destiny in Him, whether in marriage or in singleness. We bless you. We believe in 'Marriages Of Destiny!'

We would love to hear from you. Do please drop us a line and tell us how our story has encouraged you at healingpool@hotmail.co.uk .

With our sincerest blessings for your future. Philip and Kathy

# Prayer

*Lord Jesus, we come before You on behalf of every single reader of this book. You know their individual circumstances intimately. You know their destiny and You love them unconditionally.*

*We ask that You would speak to them, prepare them and lead them. Many are called by You to be married. We pray that You would remove every obstacle which the enemy has placed in their path, every obstacle they have placed, or others have put there, which is preventing the fulfilment of this desire.*

*We ask that You would lift off the discouragement which has seeded in many hearts and the pain which has started to grow and that You would ignite radical faith which will rise up in bold prayer, to contend for their own marriage partners to be released, for the hindrances to be removed and for the meetings to happen.*

*Let it happen Lord and may there be multiple good reports of Kingdom victory in this whole area of marriage and family.*

*Thank You Jesus, that You LOVE marriage and celebrate greatly over every wedding of Your friends.*

*We ask it all in Your name Jesus. Amen.*

# Some Helpful Marriage Bible Verses

**Genesis 2:22-24**
Then the LORD God made a woman from the rib he had taken out of the man, and he brought her to the man. The man said, "This is now bone of my bones and flesh of my flesh; she shall be called 'woman', for she was taken out of man." For this reason a man will leave his father and mother and be united to his wife, and they will become one flesh.

**Proverbs 12:4**
A wife of noble character is her husband's crown, but a disgraceful wife is like decay in his bones.

**Proverbs 18:22**
He who finds a wife finds what is good and receives favour from the LORD.

**Proverbs 19:14**
Houses and wealth are inherited from parents, but a prudent wife is from the LORD.

**Proverbs 31:10**
A wife of noble character who can find? She is worth far more than rubies.

**Matthew 19:4-6**
"Haven't you read," he replied, "that at the beginning the Creator 'made them male and female,' and said, 'For this reason a man will leave his father and mother and be united to his wife, and the two will become one flesh' ? So they are no longer two, but one. Therefore what God has joined together, let man not separate."

**1 Corinthians 7:1-39**
We suggest you read this in your own Bible, as the Apostle Paul talks about marriage and singleness at length.

**1 Corinthians 7 v 39**
A woman is bound to her husband as long as he lives. But if her husband dies, she is free to marry anyone she wishes, but he must belong to the Lord.

**2 Corinthians 6 v 14**
Do not be yoked together with unbelievers. For what do righteousness and wickedness have in common? Or what fellowship can light have with darkness?

**Ephesians 5:22-23**
Wives, submit to your husbands as to the Lord. For the husband is the head of the wife as Christ is the head of the church, his body, of which he is the Saviour.

**Ephesians 5:25**
Husbands love your wives, just as Christ loved the church and gave himself up for her.

**Colossians 3:18-19**
Wives, submit to your husbands, as is fitting in the Lord. Husbands, love your wives and do not be harsh with them.

**Hebrews 13:4**
Marriage should be honoured by all, and the marriage bed kept pure, for God will judge the adulterer and all the sexually immoral.

# RESOURCES

## MARRIAGE

The Marriage Book  *Nicky & Sila Lee* (2000)
God is a Matchmaker  *Derek Prince* (2003)
The Love Dare  *Stephen & Alex Kendrick* (2008)
The Mystery of Marriage  *Mike Mason* (1985)
The Marriage Covenant  *Derek Prince* (1978)
Husbands & Fathers  *Derek Prince* (2000)
Boundaries in Marriage  *Dr Henry Cloud & Dr Mark Townsend* (1999)
Fireproof  (DVD) (2009)

## HEARING GOD AND PRAYER

How to Hear God's Voice  *Mark & Patti Virkler* (2006)
Crafted Prayer  *Graham Cooke*

## HEALING

Transforming the Inner Man  *Mark & Paula Sandford* (2007)
Healing the Wounded Spirit  *Mark & Paula Sandford* (1985)
The Broken Image  *Leanne Payne* (1996)
Preparing the Way (The Story of Healing Rooms)  *Cal Pierce* (2001)
Captivating: Unveiling the Mystery of a Woman's Soul  *Mark & Stasi Eldredge* (2005)
Freedom in Christ  *Neil T Anderson* (2009)
Inside Grief  *Kathy Laity (O'Brien)* (2004)

## MINISTRIES WHICH OFFER HEALING AND HELP:

Restoring the Foundations: in depth healing and deliverance ministry
www.rtfi.org
Email: HHNOffice@RestoringTheFoundations.org

Freedom in Christ Ministries:
www.ficm.org.uk

Sozo: (healing and deliverance) Bethel Redding (Bill Johnson's church)
(Many churches internationally are also using this model)
www.bethelsozo.com

Healing Rooms: offering healing prayer
www.healingrooms.com

Ellel Ministies: ministry of healing and deliverance
www.ellelministries.org

## GENDER RELATED AND SEXUALITY ISSUES:

Setting Love in Order: Hope and Healing for the Homosexual
*Mario Berghner (1995)*

Crisis in Masculinity
*Leanne Payne (1995)*

Pursuing Sexual Wholeness: How Jesus Heals the Homosexual
*Andrew Comiskey (1989)*

Leanne Payne: Gender related issues
www.leannepayne.org

Mark Petuit: Gender related issues, successor to Leanne Payne
www.ministriesofpastoralcare.com

Lin Button
PO Box 500, Woodford Green, Essex IG8 0YB
Office answerphone: 020 8504 3966
Email: linbutton@healingprayerschool.org

Living Waters UK: (Andrew Comiskey)
PO Box 1530, London. SW1W 0WF

The Father Heart of God:
(Especially relevant if there have been shortcomings in how we were parented).

James and Denise Jordan: Father Heart Ministries
www.fatherheart.net

Peter and Heather Jackson: Father heart encounter retreats:
www.peterjackson.org

## DATING SITES/ORGANISATIONS AND FRIENDSHIP NETWORKS:

Christian Connection:
www.ChristianConnection.co.uk

The Network:
www.networkchristians.com

Christian Ramblers:
www.crc-net.org.uk

# A LITTLE BIT MORE ABOUT US:

Philip was born and has lived most of his life in Cornwall, apart from studying and working for 4 years in London. He is a chartered surveyor by profession but gave this up when God called him into the healing ministry, after miraculously healing him of a life threatening tumour. He ran a Christian centre for many years and has been pursuing a prayer and healing ministry since the mid 80s. This work now continues with Kathy.

Kathy spent several years as a missionary with Youth With A Mission, before taking a variety of jobs in the private sector. In her mid 30s she retrained as a secondary teacher of English. Following the death of her first husband she again retrained and established a Christian Life Coaching business. She was Coach for several years with the website Christian Connection. She was also involved in the Exeter healing rooms and continues to work in the healing and prayer ministry alongside Philip.

We have both been Christians over 30 years.

**To Contact Philip and Kathy Laity email: healingpool@hotmail.co.uk**